PRAYING
GOD'S WILL
for YOUR LIFE

PRAYING
GOD'S WILL
for YOUR LIFE

STORMIE OMARTIAN

THOMAS NELSON
Since 1798

NASHVILLE   DALLAS   MEXICO CITY   RIO DE JANEIRO

Published in Nashville, Tennessee, by Thomas Nelson. Thomas Nelson is a
registered trademark of Thomas Nelson, Inc.

Thomas Nelson, Inc., titles may be purchased in bulk for educational, business,
fund-raising, or sales promotional use. For information, please e-mail
SpecialMarkets@ThomasNelson.com.

Unless otherwise noted, Scripture quotations are from THE NEW KING JAMES
VERSION. © 1979, 1980, 1982, Thomas Nelson, Inc. Publishers.

Scripture quotations noted NIV are from the HOLY BIBLE: NEW
INTERNATIONAL VERSION®. © 1973, 1978, 1984 by International Bible
Society. Used by permission of Zondervan Publishing House. All rights reserved.

Scripture quotations noted NLT are from the *Holy Bible*, New Living Translation,
© 1996. Used by permission of Tyndale House Publishers, Inc., Wheaton, Illinois
60189. All rights reserved.

Some of this book's content was previously published as *Finding Peace for Your Heart*.

ISBN 978-0-8499-4684-4 (SE)

Library of Congress Cataloging-in-Publication Data

Omartian, Stormie.
   Praying God's will for your life / Stormie Omartian.
     p. cm.
   ISBN: 978-0-7852-6645-7 (TP)
    1. God—Will—meditations. 2. Christian women—Religious life.
  3. Prayer—Christianity. 4. Devotional calendars. I. Title.
   BV4527.045 2001
   248.4—dc21   2001044937

Printed in the United States of America

10 11 12 13 14 BTY 5 4 3 2 1

CONTENTS

PART TWO:
THE SOLID FOUNDATION

PART THREE:
THE OBEDIENT WALK

PART ONE

THE
INTIMATE
RELATIONSHIP

CHAPTER 1

PRAYING TO KNOW GOD'S WILL FOR YOUR LIFE

As far back as I can remember, I woke up every morning with an overwhelming sense of dread. It's the same feeling you have when you wake up for the first time after someone you love has tragically and suddenly died. The reality of it comes flooding back to you and you realize it wasn't a bad dream after all. You wish with all of your being that it was not true, but it is and you have to face it. The thought of getting through the day brings such a weight of depression it requires a major effort to even get out of bed.

That's exactly the way I always felt, even though no one had died. No one, that is, except me. I was dying on a daily basis. I could feel it, but I didn't know what to do about it.

No one ever saw my struggle, so I pretended everything was fine. And I got very good at it. I stayed as busy as possible, with as many people as possible, in order to create a diversion so grand that I didn't have to feel the terrible purposelessness of my life. But there was always that moment of extreme aloneness, with no noise and no activity, when I crossed over from sleep to consciousness. In those first waking moments, the deafening quiet exposed the futility of my life and it was unbearable.

I often thought of suicide as a means of escape because I didn't want to wake up again with that dreaded feeling and have to face another day. I certainly couldn't imagine that things could ever be any different from the way they were. I had spent a lifetime trying to transform myself and to change my circumstances, and I found I was completely powerless to do so. The way I was and the way my life was going had been entirely unacceptable to me for far too long. And I could see no other way out.

Of course I had been on an extensive search to find meaning for my life. But the god I was pursuing in my occult practices was a weak and distant god who really couldn't do anything for me unless I could be good enough, or enlightened enough, or religious enough, or smart enough to somehow get to him and prove I was worthy. I was fairly certain he had more important things to do than help me.

Realizing that I was without a god or anyone else to come to my aid, I decided it was all up to me. *I* was in charge of my destiny. *I* had to make myself acceptable to others. *I* had to make my life the way it should be. The problem was, I knew I couldn't do it.

4

I had been a singer and an actress on television for about eight years, and I was finding it increasingly difficult to hide behind either of those occupations for any length of time. The emptiness inside of me was growing at an alarming rate, and I felt so fragile that I knew it wouldn't take much for me to crack like an eggshell.

One week I was asked to sing on a series of recording sessions for a Christian musical. I was glad to have the work, and making records was far easier than the labor-intensive schedule of a television show. Back in those days we did TV shows live, so the rehearsal schedule was intense. You had to have the dance routine, dialogue, and songs you were singing down so perfectly that you wouldn't make a mistake when the cameras were rolling and you were seen live in front of millions of people.

When I arrived at the recording studio for the first session, it was filled with people, most of whom I had never met. There was a sense of peace and calm, and everyone was friendly, warm, and welcoming—quite different from what I was used to in television. My spirits began to lift immediately. This was amazing because it was an early morning session, which means I had not had much time to work out of my traditional early morning depression.

During the first break of the day I met more of the singers, musicians, and recording crew. They all had certain common qualities about them that I found very appealing: a sense of simplicity, fullness, and purpose. Someone might question how I could identify a sense of fullness, and I don't know how to explain it, except to say that it stood in stark contrast to my own emptiness. I could also sense that they were not into drugs, alcohol, and promiscuity. Again, there was that contrast.

My friend Terry was the contractor on this session, which meant she was in charge of hiring all of the singers. She was one of the best studio singers in Los Angeles, and I had worked with her often. She always sang the lead and I would stand next to her and sing second. I think she liked working with me because I never tried to compete with her. Instead, I recognized her expertise and tried to blend as well as I could with what she did. She took me under her wing at this session because she was aware that I didn't know many people there.

We were all singing three to a microphone. On our microphone, Terry was in the middle and another girl and I were on either side of her, looking off the same metal music stand. After that first break was over and we were recording again, I reached up to adjust my headphones. When I brought my hand down, the gold ring on my hand hit the metal music stand and made a loud bang. That brought the session to an immediate halt.

This was back in the days when there were none of the technological tricks studios have today. A mistake of this magnitude meant we had to start that whole section of music all over again, which was not good because it had been perfect up to that point. I feared that my recording career was over. Normally something like this could have been enough to keep me from getting called to work again. It wasn't just that I had made a mistake; it was the money it cost the producers for the time involved in having to record it all over again.

I felt badly about what happened and apologized profusely. I expected to receive angry glares, a severe shunning at lunch break, and a call asking me not to come back for the rest of the sessions. Instead, everyone acted like it was no big deal and as if they still valued me as a person. The only thing that happened was that the conductor politely said if anyone else was wearing rings or bracelets we should remove them, which we all did. I felt like crying at that point, not just because of making the mistake, but because of the love and mercy I had been shown. It was not the norm in my experience.

It was on our lunch break, when we went out together in a large group, that I learned that everyone on the session was a Christian except me. They all talked about their futures, some of which I gathered were even more precarious than mine. Yet none of them feared the future as I did. I feared I didn't have one. They knew they had one because they understood God had a plan for their lives. They said that as long as they walked in the will of God, their future was secure in His hands. I had never heard of such a thing.

Obviously their God was different from the gods I had been pursuing. He was personal. He was warm. He had a plan for each person's life. I didn't say anything about my situation because I did not want to expose that I wasn't a Christian and possibly embarrass Terry. She already knew that I was not a believer, but I didn't think that the others did. Now, looking back, I'm sure they all knew. They were probably as much aware of my emptiness as I was of their fullness.

Each day of the sessions I found myself increasingly attracted to the sense of purpose these people had about their lives. I wanted that so badly, but I didn't know how I could even get close to it. I was sure that a person must have to be born under a different star than I was in order to attain it. Yet I couldn't get the idea of God's will out of my mind.

I wonder if God has a plan for my life? I thought to myself. That would mean I didn't have to make life happen. *But what if His plan for me is to be a missionary in Siberia? Death would be better. How do I find out what God's plan is for me?*

I thought about this for the next few days of the sessions. I tried to learn more from each of the singers at every lunch break without letting them know why I was interested. I didn't want anyone *pressuring* me to have a life of purpose. Besides, being miserable was familiar to me, and I was more comfortable with what I knew.

After the last session on the final day, as I was in my car on the way home, I prayed to this God of theirs without knowing if He could even hear me. "God, if You have a will for my life," I said, "I need to know what it is and what to do about it."

I heard no reply. As I suspected, this God would probably never listen to someone like me. I went on with my life as it was, spiraling downward at an ever-increasing pace.

Over the course of the next few months many things happened to me, one of which changed my life forever: I met the

God that Terry and her friends had been talking about. The simple prayer I had prayed in the car, to a God I didn't even know, was answered.

That was thirty-one years ago, and now I know that the will of God is not some mysterious thing that only a few select people can understand. It's there for each one of us, but we have to take the necessary steps to find it. The steps are simple, but often for that very reason we don't bother to take them. Yet we *have* to take them because we can never be happy until we understand God's will for our lives and are living in it.

Until we are living in the will of God, we are destined to have lives that are unfulfilled and incomplete. Knowing that God has a plan for you gives your life purpose as nothing else can. It simplifies everything because you don't have to figure it all out and make it all happen. You just have to look to the Lord, knowing *He* has it all figured out and *He* will make it happen.

From that time on, I continually prayed, "God, tell me what to do. Show me what steps to take. Guide me where I need to go." And God answered those prayers. He spoke to my heart saying, "Just be in My presence. I'll make things happen the way they are supposed to."

In the following months and years I learned that life could be much simpler than I ever dreamed. It didn't matter what my situation was at the moment; all I had to do was take the next step the Lord was showing me. As I did, I began to see a solid way of living, which I could explain to other people. I could say, "You just take these steps. As long as you are walking with God and living His way, you are not likely to get off the path. And if by chance you do, He will get you right back on. That's because you've been listening to God's voice and you will feel in your heart when you violate one of His directions."

The following chapters in this book are the basic steps to take to establish an intimate relationship with God, to lay a solid foundation in His truth, and to learn the basic principles of obedience. All of these things *are* the will of God for your life, as revealed in His Word, and you must do them in order to be *in* the will of God.

At the end of each chapter are short prayers and a section called Tools of Truth. These are Scripture verses that are God's truth for your life. You can claim them as God's will for you, and they will give you security and confidence.

I suggest that you pray for yourself every day for a month, using each one of the twenty areas of prayer focus I have included in this book. Pray a chapter a day for a twenty-day prayerful walk to spiritual well-being.

Now let me tell you about each of these steps and how I learned of their importance in our lives.

CHAPTER 2

PRAYING TO KNOW
GOD AS A
POWERFUL PRESENCE

I took the handful of sleeping pills a friend had just given me and added them to my growing collection in a little gold box in the back of the bottom drawer of my bedroom dresser. "I have nearly enough to do the job right this time," I told myself. Deliberately and methodically I planned my suicide. I wanted to make it look like an accidental overdose so my sister and dad wouldn't bear any guilt.

I had tried to kill myself when I was fourteen by downing an odd combination of drugs in our bathroom, but they only succeeded in making me very sick. Since that failed attempt, I had thrown myself into everything I could possibly find to get out of my dark, emotional prison cell. Unfortunately, every so-called "key to life" I tried only led me closer to death and farther from the freedom, peace, and release I so desperately sought.

I'd had plenty of good psychiatric and psychological counseling, especially if measured in terms of how much money I had paid, and I was grateful for each doctor as he kept me from destroying myself. Yet at twenty-eight years old, fourteen years after my suicide attempt, I still felt as if I were down in a dark hole, and I couldn't produce the strength to pick myself up one more time. Death was again the only solution I could see. I was amazed that in all those years of struggle my life had still come to nothing.

At that low point, which was a few months after the series of recording sessions, my friend Terry said, "I can see you're not doing well, Stormie. Won't you come with me and talk to my pastor?" Sensing my reluctance, she quickly added, "You've got nothing to lose."

I silently bore witness to her accurate assessment of my situation and agreed to go even though I wanted nothing whatsoever to do with any kind of religion. My experience with churches had been that they made me feel more dead than I did already.

Terry took me to meet Pastor Jack Hayford from the nearby Church on the Way, and it turned out to be like no other meeting I'd ever had. We met him at a restaurant for lunch, and from the moment he started talking, he had my full attention. He asked me a little about myself, but I was not open to revealing anything of my desperate circumstances.

Even at this late hour in my life, I wanted to appear successful. For more than an hour, Pastor Jack talked about God the way someone talks about a best friend. He said that at my invitation, God would come to live within me and transform my life from the inside out.

"If you receive Jesus, the relationship you can have with God will be so personal that every part of your being can be shared with Him and His with you," Pastor Jack explained. "You would never be without hope or purpose again."

I had no trouble listening to him talk about God because I knew there was a spirit realm. I had seen enough supernatural manifestations through my delving into the occult to convince me of their reality. But when he started talking about receiving Jesus and being born again, I winced.

I had frequently seen people standing on street corners, waving black books and screaming, "Jesus saves!" and "You're all going to hell!" to everyone passing by. Because of them, I feared that accepting Jesus meant having an intellectual lobotomy, which would turn me into an unthinking, self-righteous, coldhearted, beat-people-over-the-head-with-your-Bible kind of person with whom the reality of other people's true pain and circumstances never registered. I had noticed, however, that neither Pastor Jack nor Terry was anything like that.

Fortunately, Pastor Jack saw through my fears and didn't push me for any commitment. Instead he sent me home with three books: the first, about the life of Jesus, was the gospel of John in book form; the second one, *The Screwtape Letters* by

C. S. Lewis, was about the reality of evil; and the third was a book about the working of the Holy Spirit of God in people's lives.

"Let's talk again next week in my office and you can let me know then what you think of these books," Pastor Jack said as we ended our meeting. We agreed, and I went home to start reading. Something about what Terry and Pastor Jack said and did that day made me want to find out what they knew that I didn't.

As I read the pages of each book, I realized that for years I had believed lies about Jesus, judging Him from what I'd heard of Him without really *knowing* Him. His name and reputation had been so maligned, mocked, misinterpreted, misconstrued, joked and lied about for so long that I dismissed Him from any possible connection with my life. As I read I also realized that God was not the cold and distant force I had thought, but rather a loving and powerful Father who sent us a means of total restoration through Jesus, His Son.

The more I read, the more I saw that my New Age belief that there is no evil in the world except what exists in people's minds was a deception. As C. S. Lewis's book dramatized the activity of Satan, the source of the horrible things that happen to people became obvious. There *is* an evil force intent on our destruction, and Satan, the head of that force, is real and very much our enemy.

As I seriously pondered all I read, I also thought about Terry and Pastor Jack and how much I admired them. They were not phony, stupid, or unloving. They had an inherent, simple beauty and a bold confidence that radiated God's power because they had acknowledged Him as Lord of their lives.

THE MOST IMPORTANT STEP
YOU'LL EVER TAKE

All of us need to acknowledge God, recognize that He is on our side, and let Him be Lord over our lives.

The prophet Jeremiah asked God a question we all ask: "Why then is there no healing for the wound of my people?" (Jer. 8:22 NIV).

And God answered, "They go from one sin to another; they do not acknowledge me" (Jer. 9:3 NIV).

One of the main reasons people are lonely and distressed is that they have not acknowledged God as Savior, as Father, as Holy Spirit, as Lord in every area of life, and as the Name who answers every need. Until we have aligned ourselves properly with God, nothing in life will fall into place as it should.

As I read those books I realized that God would be there for me if I needed Him. I acknowledged God's presence in my life, and I looked forward to my next meeting with Pastor Jack and Terry.

Not long afterward, I was browsing in a Christian bookstore and came across a charming children's book called *Three in One* by Joanne Marxhausen.[1] The author used the example of an apple with its three parts—the peel, the flesh, and the core—to point out that those three parts were still just one apple. Likewise, she described three aspects of God: the Father, the Son, and the Holy Spirit. Three parts, but only one God. The message of this simple illustration was so clear that I realized we can never truly know God until we know Him in all those ways.

If you have never acknowledged God's presence in your life, you might want to do so now by praying the first prayer below. If you have done so in the past, you may want to renew your commitment to God by praying the second prayer.

PRAYERS

TO ACKNOWLEDGE GOD'S PRESENCE
Lord, I have not recognized You as the God of the universe. Forgive me for that mistake. Help me sense Your presence so strongly in my life that I never doubt it.

TO RENEW YOUR AWARENESS OF GOD'S PRESENCE
Lord, I know You are God of the universe, and I recognize that You are present in my life. Please help me sense Your hand on me as I go about my daily tasks. I love You, Lord, and I thank You for Your love and care for me.

TOOLS OF TRUTH

I am with you always, even to the end of the age.

MATTHEW 28:20 NLT

In all your ways acknowledge Him,
And He shall direct your paths.

PROVERBS 3:6

The fear of the LORD is a fountain of life.

PROVERBS 14:27

For whatever is born of God overcomes the world.

1 JOHN 5:4

You are my Lord,
My goodness is nothing apart from You.

PSALM 16:2

If God is for us, who can be against us?

ROMANS 8:31

CHAPTER 3

PRAYING TO
KNOW GOD AS
YOUR SAVIOR

As I read the books Pastor Jack gave me, I could immediately see two reasons to acknowledge Jesus as my Savior. *The first reason was to be completely free of guilt.*

My sense of guilt was overwhelming, but for all the wrong reasons. I had no remorse for things I *did* that were wrong. I saw actions like lying and love affairs as means of survival and refused to allow myself to feel bad about them. Whenever I did feel guilty, I assumed it was because my mother had instilled it in me with her constant anger. She had a way of making everything I did seem evil; some days I even felt guilty for being alive.

I have told the story of my mother's abuse in my book *Stormie* and in *Lord, I Want to Be Whole*, my book about emotional healing. I will not recount it completely here, but for you to understand how I was feeling, you need to know that my mother sometimes locked me in a small, rectangular storage area underneath the stairs where the dirty laundry was kept in an old wicker basket. Whenever she did, she would scream, "You're worthless, and you'll never amount to anything!"

I was never really sure what I had done to warrant being locked in the closet, but I knew it must be bad. I knew I must be bad, and I believed that all the negative things she ever said about me were surely accurate. After all, she was my mother.

Everyone has some kind of guilt for mistakes of the past. Sometimes it's for things we know we've done; sometimes it's deep regret over what we fear we could have prevented; and sometimes it's for violation of certain natural laws we're not even aware of violating. Whatever the reason, the load of guilt sits on us with crushing weight, and unless it's eliminated it separates us from the fullness of life.

What can ever take our guilt away? Consider, for instance, the man who accidentally backed a car over his two-year-old daughter and killed her. Or the woman who took drugs when she was pregnant and gave birth to a brain-damaged child. What about the mother who accidentally shot and killed her teenage son when he came home late one night and she thought he was a robber? How do these people find freedom from guilt over such devastating and irreparable damage?

Or how do you and I live with painful regrets? *If only*

I'd . . . ; If I just hadn't . . . These thoughts echo the agony of situations that can never be changed. It's done! And there's no way to live with the truth of it unless you push it down deep and never allow yourself to feel it again. Don't talk about it. Don't bring it up. The trouble with that is you think you're getting away with it until it starts to surface on its own. But then it comes out in the form of a disease. Or perhaps it affects your mind and emotions, making you angry or withdrawn or phobic or depressed.

How do you and I live with our guilty feelings over things that aren't our fault, but we fear *might* be? "If I'd been more obedient, maybe my dad wouldn't have left us." "Did I drive my husband to have that affair?" "If only I hadn't let my teenage daughter go out that night, she'd never have been hit by a drunk driver." Guilt upon guilt piles up to become a burden that is literally *unbearable*.

Finally, what about our guilt over things we've done that violated God's laws, laws of which we weren't even aware at the time? No matter how much a woman who has had an abortion believes her decision was right, I've never heard one say, "I've been fulfilled and enriched by this experience." She may feel relieved of a burden, but she never thinks, *What a wonderful thing I've done. I know I have truly realized God's purpose for my life and I am a better person because of it.* Whether she acknowledges it or not, the guilt is there because she has violated a law of nature.

What or who can take this guilt away? A friend's saying,

"Don't worry about it . . . It wasn't your fault . . . You can't blame yourself," never gets rid of what you feel inside. Only God's forgiveness can do that. When we receive Jesus, we are immediately released from the penalty for our past mistakes. For the first time in my life I felt free from having to face the failure of my past on a moment-to-moment basis.

The second important reason to receive Jesus was to have the peace of knowing that my future was secure. And not only is my eternal future secure—Jesus said anyone who believes in Him will have everlasting life (John 6:40)—but my future in *this* life is also secure. God promises that if we acknowledge Him, He will guide us safely where we need to go (Prov. 3:6). This doesn't mean that we will instantly have all of our problems solved and never again know pain, but we will have the power within us to reach our full potential. We can never find any greater security than that.

LIFE BEFORE DEATH

When Jesus died on the cross, He also rose from the dead to break the power of death over anyone who receives His life. Jesus conquered death—whether at the end of our lives or in the multiple ways that we face death daily. In the death of our dreams, finances, health, or relationships, Jesus can bring His life to resurrect those dead places in us. Therefore we don't have to feel hopeless. He also gives to everyone who opens up to Him a *quality* of life that is meaningful, abundant, and fulfilling. He transcends our every limitation and boundary and enables us to do things we never would have been capable of aside from Him. He is the only one with power and authority over the emotions or bondage that torture us. He is the only one who can give us life *before* death as well as life hereafter. Without Him we die a little every day. With Him we become more and more alive.

When Terry and I met with Pastor Jack the week following our first meeting, he asked me directly, "Well, what did you think of the books I gave you?"

"I think they are the truth," I responded with uncharacteristic confidence.

"So would you like to receive God's life in you?" he asked openly.

"Yes," I said without hesitation. "I want that, and I want all that God has for me."

That day in October of 1970, I decided to believe Jesus was who He said He was and receive Him into my life.

After I prayed that prayer with Pastor Jack, Terry and I were leaving the office when he caught the arm of a young man walking by.

"Stormie, I want you to meet Paul, my assistant pastor," he said. "Tell him what just happened."

I was uneasy as I shook Paul's hand and said sheepishly, "I just received Jesus."

I half expected him to laugh and say, "You've got to be kidding!" Much to my amazement he said with a reassuring combination of sincerity and seriousness, "Praise God. That's wonderful." I smiled in response and it felt good.

There is release in telling someone you have received Jesus. It doesn't matter who. All that matters is that you have acknowledged Jesus to someone else so that it is firmly established. Even if you've known the Lord for a long time, it's good to do that frequently. Your belief in Him needs to be reconfirmed periodically. Remind yourself that the resurrection life of Jesus lives *in* you and that He is able to raise up any dead areas of your life.

It's also good to write the date you received the Lord in your Bible or a record book that will not be thrown away. This records your new birth date so that if you ever have doubt or confusion about whether it really happened, you will have it written in black and white. One of my friends was born again six or seven times because her emotions were fragile and her mind so clouded with oppression that she was never sure she had done it well enough the first time. That isn't necessary.

You are never born again by chance. When you receive Jesus, it is because God the Father is drawing you in. Jesus said, "No one can come to Me unless the Father who sent Me draws him" (John 6:44). Once God draws you in, it's done—once and for all. You are released from guilt, your future is secure, and you are saved from death in every part of your life.

Christianity is a living relationship with God through Jesus, His Son. *Salvation* is not just something Jesus did for us; it is Jesus living in us. You may have been born into a

Christian family or have attended a Christian church all your life, but if you haven't told God that you want to receive Jesus, you haven't been born into the kingdom of God. You can't inherit it, get it by osmosis, transplant it, implant it—or wish upon a star for it. You have to declare your faith before the Lord.

After I became a Christian, I began to talk to my friends about my experience, particularly my best friend, Diane. We had always been so close, and now we could not share the most important experience in my life. We had been into the occult together, and she thought I was crazy to get involved in this "Jesus thing." One day, however, she called me and was very depressed.

"The Lord would really make a difference in your life," I told her. "Jesus isn't like the gods we studied in the occult. Those gods don't have the power to set us free. Jesus does. He can set you free from your depression."

Apparently I convinced her of the major difference the Lord had made in my life, because she asked me to pray with her to receive Jesus as her Savior. It was the first time I had ever led anyone to the Lord, and I was nervous about whether I was doing it right. But I had heard Pastor Jack lead people to the Lord in his touching way, and so I remembered some of the things he said. The prayer on the next page is similar to the one I asked her to pray. If you want to receive Jesus into your life, you can pray this same prayer also.

PRAYERS

TO RECEIVE JESUS AS SAVIOR

Jesus, I acknowledge You this day. I believe You are the Son of God as You say You are. Although it's hard to comprehend love so great, I believe You laid down Your life for me so that I might have life eternally and abundantly now. I ask You to forgive me for not living Your way. I need You to help me become all You created me to be. Come into my life and fill me with Your Holy Spirit. Let all the death in me be crowded out by the power of Your presence, and this day turn my life into a new beginning.

If you don't feel comfortable with this prayer, then talk to Jesus as you would to a good friend, and confess you've made some mistakes. Tell Him you can't live without Him. Ask Him to forgive you and to come into your heart. Tell Him you receive Him as Lord, and thank Him for His eternal life and forgiveness.

If you wish to renew your commitment to Your Savior, pray the following prayer:

TO RENEW YOUR COMMITMENT TO JESUS AS YOUR SAVIOR

Jesus, I acknowledge Your presence in my life. I know that You live in me because I have accepted You as Savior. I know that You died for me and You are able to raise up the dead areas of my life. Show me where I am not walking fully in all You have for me. I make a new commitment to living Your way.

TOOLS OF TRUTH

And we have seen and testify that the Father has sent the Son as Savior of the world. Whoever confesses that Jesus is the Son of God, God abides in him, and he in God.

1 JOHN 4:14–15

Jesus said to him, "I am the way, the truth, and the life. No one comes to the Father except through Me."

JOHN 14:6

Nor is there salvation in any other, for there is no other name under heaven given among men by which we must be saved.

ACTS 4:12

Unless one is born again, he cannot see the kingdom of God.

JOHN 3:3

If you confess with your mouth the Lord Jesus and believe in your heart that God has raised Him from the dead, you will be saved.

ROMANS 10:9

CHAPTER 4

PRAYING TO KNOW GOD AS YOUR HEAVENLY FATHER

Acknowledging God as heavenly Father is sometimes difficult for people, especially if they didn't have a father or have been mistreated by a male parent or authority figure.

One young woman told me, "Don't talk to me about God being a father. My father forced me to have sex with him until I left home, and now I'm unable to have a normal relationship with any man at all." Another confided to me, "My father beat me every time he came home drunk, and now I hate him. How can I think of God as a father?" A middle-aged man said, "My father never did anything for me. He was a weakling. He contributed nothing to my life and then eventually deserted us. Don't mention the word *father*."

I never had a dad who abused me, and for that I am very grateful. Yet my dad never rescued me from my abusive mother, and he was the only one with the power and authority to do so. Because of that experience, I subconsciously felt God would not help me either. I didn't openly rebel against or resent God; instead I just felt forgotten.

Your life experiences may cause you to feel as these people did. But let me assure you that God will never be a father who comes home drunk, hides behind a newspaper, beats you, molests you, lies to you, betrays you, deserts you, or is too busy for you. He is different. He is a father who "knows the things you have need of" (Matt. 6:8) and will "give good things to those who ask Him" (Matt. 7:11). He will never leave nor forsake you, He will unfailingly have your best interest in mind, and He will always have more for you than you ever dreamed of for yourself.

Examine your relationship with the heavenly Father and see if any of the following statements apply to you:

- "I doubt that I am a beloved son or daughter to my heavenly Father."

- "I feel distant from Him."

- "I am afraid of Him."

- "I am angry with Him."

- "I feel abandoned by Him."

- "The thought of my heavenly Father brings tears of pain rather than feelings of joy."

If any one of these statements applies to you, you definitely need a greater understanding of your heavenly Father's love for you. Ask Him to make it clear. Pray the prayer at the end of this chapter. And then determine that you will not close yourself off from the Father who loves you. Give Him a chance to prove Himself faithful and show His power in your behalf.

In my new relationship with God, I was strongly aware of His love, especially His love for *other* people, but I didn't believe that He loved *me* as much as He loved *them*. The enormity of residual hurt and unforgiveness from the past, along with guilt, sadness, and fear, all served as a giant barrier that kept me from feeling His love. Because of these things, acknowledging God as *Father* took a great step of faith.

It's one thing to know Jesus; it's another to know the Father. Salvation's purpose is not only to get us to Christ, but also to get us to the Father, where we understand our relationship with our Creator. We may have distorted images of Him because of everything that has happened to us, but we will not be able to see who *we* really are until we are able to see God as *He* really is. Then, out of the context of a relationship that secures and satisfies us, we can begin to grow. There is much healing ahead for us when we do.

If you want to begin this process, or to renew your relationship with your heavenly father, say one of the following prayers:

PRAYERS

TO KNOW GOD AS YOUR HEAVENLY FATHER
God, I acknowledge You as my heavenly Father today. Heal any misconception I have of You. Where my earthly father has failed me and I have blamed You, forgive me and take away that hurt. I long to receive the inheritance that You have promised Your children.

If you know God as your Father, but feel distant from Him at times, pray the following prayer:

TO RENEW YOUR RELATIONSHIP WITH GOD AS FATHER
Lord, I know You are my heavenly Father and You love me as no one else can. But sometimes I cannot feel Your unconditional love for me. Help me understand the truth of Your Word in my life today. And help me draw closer to You.

TOOLS OF TRUTH

I will be a Father to you,
And you shall be My sons and daughters,
Says the LORD Almighty.

2 CORINTHIANS 6:18

As a father has compassion on his children,
so the LORD has compassion on those who fear him.

PSALM 103:13 NIV

Do not fear, little flock, for it is your Father's good pleasure
to give you the kingdom.

LUKE 12:32

You, O LORD, are our Father;
Our Redeemer from Everlasting is Your name.

ISAIAH 63:16

For the Father judges no one, but has committed all judgment to the Son.

JOHN 5:22

CHAPTER 5

PRAYING TO KNOW
GOD AS THE
HOLY SPIRIT

When I first heard the names Helper and Comforter in reference to the Holy Spirit, I knew immediately I wanted those attributes of God in my life. I realized that to get them, I first had to acknowledge the Holy Spirit's existence and then be open to His working in me. When I did that, I learned three important reasons to be filled with God's Holy Spirit:

- to worship God more fully

- to experience and communicate God's love more completely

- to appropriate God's power in my life more effectively

If you acknowledge Jesus as Savior and God as Father, you have to acknowledge the Holy Spirit. I've heard certain Christians speak of the Trinity as Father, Son, and H-H-L-L-S-S-P-P-S-S-H-H. They can hardly say "Holy Spirit" without choking, let alone acknowledge His working in their lives. Perhaps it's because they know too little about Him. Or maybe they were in a situation in which odd things were done in the name of the Holy Spirit. (Or perhaps they heard the term "Holy Ghost" and were afraid of ghosts!) Whatever the reason, let me assure you that the Holy Spirit is the Spirit of God sent by Jesus to give us comfort, to build us up, to guide us in all truth, to bring us spiritual gifts, to help us pray more effectively, to give us wisdom and revelation, and to help us know God's will for our lives. Are there people who can honestly say they don't ever need those things?

The Holy Spirit cannot be ignored. We can't pretend He doesn't exist or say that Jesus didn't mean it when He promised He would send the Holy Spirit to us, or suggest that God was just kidding when He said He was pouring out His Spirit on all humankind. The Holy Spirit is not a vapor or a mystical cloud; He is another part of God. (Remember the peel, the flesh, and the core of the apple?) He is God's power and the means by which God speaks to us. If we ignore or reject Him, we will cut off this power and communication from working in our lives.

If your lips can say, "Jesus is Lord," you can be sure the Spirit of God is working in your life already. Being filled with the Spirit is mentioned in many scriptures. Since there seem to be just as many interpretations of them as there are denominations, I'm not going to confine you to mine. Simply ask the Holy Spirit what those scriptures should mean to you, and leave it in His hands to tell you.

The Bible says, "I will put My Spirit within you and cause you to walk in My statutes, and you will keep My judgments and do them" (Ezek. 36:27). The Holy Spirit works the wholeness of God into us. And there need be no fear or mystery about this, because we alone of God's creation have a special place built in us where His Spirit can reside. That place will always be empty until it is filled with Him.

We don't want to have "a form of godliness" but deny "its power" (2 Tim. 3:5); denying God's power limits what God can do in our lives and prevents us from moving into all God has for us. Nor do we want to be "always learning and never able to come to the knowledge of the truth" (2 Tim. 3:7). Unless the Holy Spirit coaches us from within, our knowledge of the truth will always be limited, and our spiritual health will be incomplete. Don't limit what God can do in you by failing to acknowledge His Holy Spirit in your life.

I have discovered over the years, however, that the infilling of the Holy Spirit is ongoing and ever deepening. We have to be willing to open up to each new level and dimension so that He can enable us to accomplish what we could never do without this full measure of His love, power, and life.

No matter how long you have known the Lord, it's good to pray the following prayer to Him frequently:

PRAYER

God, help me understand all I need to know about You and the workings of Your Spirit in my life. Fill me with Your Holy Spirit in a fresh new way this day, and work powerfully in me.

TOOLS OF TRUTH

And I will pray the Father, and He will give you another Helper, that He may abide with you forever—the Spirit of truth, whom the world cannot receive, because it neither sees Him nor knows Him; but you know Him, for He dwells with you and will be in you.

JOHN 14:16–17

If you then, being evil, know how to give good gifts to your children, how much more will your heavenly Father give the Holy Spirit to those who ask Him!

LUKE 11:13

However, when He, the Spirit of truth, has come, He will guide you into all truth; for He will not speak on His own authority, but whatever He hears He will speak; and He will tell you things to come.

JOHN 16:13

Repent, and let every one of you be baptized in the name of Jesus Christ for the remission of sins; and you shall receive the gift of the Holy Spirit. For the promise is to you and to your children, and to all who are afar off, as many as the Lord our God will call.

ACTS 2:38–39

CHAPTER 6

PRAYING TO KNOW GOD AS LORD OVER EVERY AREA OF YOUR LIFE

Once I'd begun to know God as Savior, as Father, and as Holy Spirit, I found I needed to expose many areas of my life to His influence. This was difficult because it called for my deepening trust. Until then I'd had few positive experiences when someone other than myself was in control of my life.

In every house I lived in when I was growing up, we always had rooms that no one was allowed to see. They contained a confusing clutter of items rendered useless by their overwhelming number and lack of order. One reason my mother never wanted anyone to come to our house (aside from the fact that it was too exhausting for her to keep up a front of normalcy) was that she was afraid someone would see the secret rooms. These rooms were reflective of our family life. The secret of my mother's mental illness had to be hidden at all costs. When I grew up, it was as if those secret rooms in our home became secret places in my heart. I kept so many parts of me hidden that I lived in terror that they would be discovered and I'd be rejected.

When I first received Jesus into my heart, I showed Him into the guest room. The problem was, He wasn't content to stay there. He kept knocking on one door after another until I was opening doors to rooms I had never even known were there. He exposed every dark corner of each room to His cleansing light. I soon realized that He wanted me to acknowledge Him as Lord over *every* area of my life.

One such room in my heart was the issue of having children. I married my husband, Michael, about three years after I received Jesus, and because so much was happening in our lives at that time, we never really discussed children. I had a million reasons for not wanting any, not the least of which was the fear that I would perpetuate my own crippled upbringing. I couldn't bear to watch myself destroy an innocent life. As God knocked on one door after another—finances, marriage, attitudes, appearance, friendships—I opened up to His lordship. Yet I turned a deaf ear as He tapped relentlessly at the door of motherhood, which was dead-bolted by my selfishness and fear. The knocking persisted, however, challenging my daily "Jesus, be Lord over every area of my life" prayer.

One morning about a year after we were married, friends stopped us before church to show off their new son. As I held him briefly, I had a vision of holding a child of my own. Later in church I thought about that moment, and the possibility of having a baby suddenly seemed pleasant.

Okay, Lord, I thought, *if we're really supposed to have a child, let me hear something to that effect from Michael.* With that I put the matter totally out of my mind.

Later that afternoon, Michael turned to me and said, "That baby you were holding this morning before church was so cute. Maybe we should have one of our own."

"What?" I said in disbelief. "Are you serious?"

"Sure. Why not? Isn't that what people do?" he asked.

"Yes, but I've never heard you say anything like that before."

Remembering my quick prayer that morning, I prayed silently, *Lord, it's frightening how fast You can work sometimes. May Your perfect will be done in my life.*

Even though I was still fearful and apprehensive, I knew the time had come when God was going to bring life to a place in me that had died years before. I sensed that allowing Him to be Lord over this area would be a major part of the redemption of all that had been lost in my life.

GIVING HIM THE RUN OF THE HOUSE

When you invite Jesus into the home of your being (being born again), you are supposed to also give Him the run of the house (making Him Lord over your life). However, many of us are slow to do that completely. Whether we admit it or not, we hesitate to believe that God can be trusted with *every* area of our lives.

The Bible says,

> Trust in the LORD with *all* your heart,
> And lean not on your own understanding;
> In *all* your ways acknowledge Him,
> And He shall direct your paths.
>
> (Prov. 3:5–6, emphasis added)

Notice that word *all*. It's very specific. If we want things to work out well, we have to acknowledge Him as Lord over *all* areas of our lives. I had to be willing to give God the right-of-way by frequently saying, "Jesus, be Lord over every area of my life." Then as He pointed to places where I had not opened the door to His rulership, I let Him in.

I know now that God does this with all people who invite Him to dwell in their lives. Some people give Him total access to the home of their being right away. Others leave Him standing in the entryway indefinitely. Many people do as I did and allow Him to gain entrance slowly. When He knocks on different doors inside you, just know that He will never bulldoze His way in and break down the walls. He will simply knock persistently and quietly and, as He's invited, will come to gently occupy each corner of your life to clean and rebuild.

In Jesus' time on earth He touched dead bodies and restored them to life. He also touched lepers and restored them to health. He will do as much for you right now. He will never say, "You are untouchable to Me; you are too far gone; you smell too bad; your failure is too great; your circumstances are too dead."

If something has died in you or your life, God is moved by compassion for it. Wherever there are dead places in you, He will breathe life into them. He cares about your feelings and weaknesses. He desires to touch you with healing and life, but He will not do it unless you first acknowledge Him as Lord over those areas and invite Him into the situation. The fact that He won't touch those areas without an invitation from you is not an indication that He doesn't care; rather, He has given you a choice. Will you choose to open up and share every part of yourself with Him and let Him reign in your life?

When my husband and I lived in California, we had a house that was open, with few walls on the inside. People would tell me, "When I come into your house, I can't just stay in the entryway. I have to walk into the living room, kitchen, or den." Because of the lack of barriers, the home itself invited them to move through it. I believe this reflects the way our relationship with God is supposed to be. When the barriers are down, He is not restricted from going into any area He desires. That means we are open to whatever God wants to do in us, no matter how uncomfortable it may feel at the time. The happiest people I know put all of their lives into God's hands, knowing that wherever He is enthroned, no threat of hell can succeed against them.

Acknowledging God as Lord over every area of your life is an ongoing act of will. Because of that, I recommend saying a short prayer like this every morning when you wake up:

PRAYER

God, I acknowledge You as Lord over every area of my life this day. Help me walk in Your perfect will in all that I do and everything that I say.

TOOLS OF TRUTH

Therefore God also has highly exalted Him and given Him the name which is above every name, that at the name of Jesus every knee should bow, of those in heaven, and of those on earth, and of those under the earth, and that every tongue should confess that Jesus Christ is Lord, to the glory of God the Father.

PHILIPPIANS 2:9–11

You call Me Teacher and Lord, and you say well, for so I am.

JOHN 13:13

For if we live, we live to the Lord; and if we die, we die to the Lord. Therefore, whether we live or die, we are the Lord's.

ROMANS 14:8

Jesus said to him, "You shall love the LORD your God with all your heart, with all your soul, and with all your mind."

MATTHEW 22:37

Trust in the LORD with all your heart,
And lean not on your own understanding.

PROVERBS 3:5

CHAPTER 7

PRAYING TO KNOW GOD AS A NAME THAT ANSWERS YOUR EVERY NEED

A few weeks before I had that talk with Terry about meeting her pastor, I woke in the middle of the night choking back sobs and gasping for breath. Feelings of desperate loneliness swept over me like that of being lost in the dark as a child, and I had a sense of some strange overpowering and suffocating, death-like presence in the room with me. I jolted to a sitting position to see, much to my relief, that I was safe in my own bed.

"Thank God, it's not real," I cried into my hands as I tried to massage away memories of the all-too-familiar dream.

Part of the emotional torment of the years before I came to the Lord was recurring nightmares so genuine that when I awoke from them it took time to determine what was reality and what was not. In these frightening dreams, I was in a big, dark, empty room that grew larger and larger until I was overwhelmed and engulfed with paralyzing fear. The gripping despair I felt from these nightmares became so intense that gradually it carried over into the daytime as well.

When I shared these events with Terry, she gave me what seemed at the time to be very odd advice.

"When that happens," she instructed me, "just speak the name of Jesus over and over. It will take the fear away."

"That's it?" I replied, doubtful yet willing to do anything she said if it would help. We had not discussed the Lord much before, so this suggestion seemed very foreign.

I didn't think much about our conversation until the next time I woke out of a nightmare and immediately remembered Terry's advice.

"Jesus," I whispered as I gasped for air. "Jesus!" I called louder and held my breath for a moment. "Jesus, Jesus, Jesus," I said again and again as though clinging for life to the sound of that word. In a few minutes the fear lifted.

It's just as she predicted, I thought to myself in amazement as I rolled over and went back to sleep.

That was my first experience with the power of Jesus' name, and I have never forgotten it. If His name had that much effect over the realm of darkness for someone who was not even acquainted with Him, imagine the power of His name for those who know and love Him.

A NAME FOR ALL SEASONS

Certain guarantees and rewards are inherent in simply acknowledging the name of Jesus. For example, the Bible says,

"The name of the LORD is a strong tower; the righteous run to it and are safe" (Prov. 18:10).

There is a covering of protection over anyone who turns to the name of the Lord. That's why my saying His name over and over—not in a mindless chanting but crying out to Him for help—brought the kingdom of His life to bear upon mine. It's true I had not at that point received Him as Savior, but I was being drawn to Him, as the events of several weeks later proved.

The Lord has many names in the Bible, and each one expresses an aspect of His nature or one of His attributes. When we acknowledge Him by those names, we invite Him to be those things to us. For example, He is called Healer. When we pray, "Jesus, You are my Healer," and mix it with faith, it brings this attribute to bear upon our lives.

One of the reasons we do not have the wholeness, fulfillment, and peace we desire is that we have not acknowledged God as the answer to our every need. We think, *He may have given me eternal life, but I don't know if He can handle my financial problems.* Or we think, *I know He can lead me to a better job, but I'm not sure if He can mend this marriage.* Or, *He healed my back, but I don't know if He can take away my depression.* The truth is, He is *everything* we need, and we have to remember that always. In fact, it's good to tell yourself daily, "God is everything I need," and then say the name of the Lord that answers your specific need at that moment.

Do you need hope? He is called our Hope. Pray, "Jesus, You are my Hope."

Are you weak? He is called our Strength. Pray, "Jesus, You are my Strength."

Do you need advice? He is called Counselor. Pray, "Jesus, You are my Counselor."

Do you feel oppressed? He is called Deliverer.

Are you lonely? He is called Companion and Friend.

He is also called Emmanuel, which means "God with us." He is not some distant, cold being with no interest in you. He is Emmanuel, the God who is with you right now to the degree you acknowledge Him in your life.

I have listed thirty of the biblical names of the Lord on page 53. Read that list over, keeping in mind that God desires to be all those things to you. Every day you can, choose at least one name that is applicable to your needs and frequently thank God that He is that for you. Acknowledging that He *is* these things is the first step toward the realization of His becoming them in your life. Keep in mind that everything about *His* personality is stronger than anything negative in *yours*.

IN ORDER TO KNOW HIM BETTER

Another good reason to acknowledge the name of the Lord is that Jesus says if we acknowledge Him, He will acknowledge us. And there is an intimacy that grows as long as this acknowledgment is sustained.

When my mother locked me in the closet for hours at a time, I felt helpless and afraid. "They've forgotten me," I

THIRTY ATTRIBUTES OF THE LORD

1. He is my Restorer (Ps. 23:3).
2. He is my Helper (John 14:16).
3. He is my Strength (Isa. 12:2).
4. He is my Redeemer (Isa. 59:20).
5. He is my Hope (Ps. 71:5).
6. He is my Patience (Rom. 15:5).
7. He is my Truth (John 14:6).
8. He is my Resting Place (Jer. 50:6).
9. He is my Overcomer (John 16:33).
10. He is my Light (John 8:12).
11. He is the Power of God (1 Cor. 1:24).
12. He is my Bread of Life (John 6:35).
13. He is my Fortress (Ps. 18:2).
14. He is my Refuge from the Storm (Isa. 25:4).
15. He is my Everlasting Father (Isa. 9:6).
16. He is the Author of My Faith (Heb. 12:2).
17. He is my Deliverer (Ps. 70:5).
18. He is my Counselor (Ps. 16:7).
19. He is my Peace (Eph. 2:14).
20. He is my Rewarder (Heb. 11:6).
21. He is my Healer (Mal. 4:2).
22. He is my Shield (Ps. 33:20).
23. He is my Wisdom of God (1 Cor. 1:24).
24. He is my Purifier (Mal. 3:3).
25. He is my Hiding Place (Ps. 32:7).
26. He is my Shade from the Heat (Isa. 25:4).
27. He is my Refiner (Mal. 3:2–3).
28. He is my Resurrection (John 11:25).
29. He is the Lifter of My Head (Ps. 3:3).
30. He is my Stronghold in the Day of Trouble (Nah. 1:7).

cried to myself. "No one remembers I'm here." So it wasn't surprising when I later became fearful that God would forget me too. I felt as King David did: "For there is no one who acknowledges me; refuge has failed me; no one cares for my soul" (Ps. 142:4).

Sometimes we feel that no one knows or cares who we really are. But God knows and cares. One common question from people who have been abused is, "Where was God when the abuse happened?" The answer is that *God is where He is asked to be*. He knew and cared that I was locked in that closet. Yet it wasn't until years later when I asked Him that He released me and healed me of its effects. It would have happened sooner if I had received Him and made Him Lord over my life sooner. No matter who has deserted or failed us in one way or another in the past, the Lord will always be there for us today. The Bible says, "When my father and my mother forsake me, then the LORD will take care of me" (Ps. 27:10). Those words are particularly meaningful if your mother or father has, in fact, abused, disappointed, or forsaken you. The Lord, however, will never let us down or forget us.

Jesus said when you know the truth, you will be set free. I always thought that meant knowing the truth of a situation, but actually it is knowing *God's* truth in every situation. And our eyes will never be opened to His truth until our hearts are fully opened to Him and we acknowledge Him as everything we need. For that *is* God's will for our lives.

PRAYERS

Jesus, thank You that You are Emmanuel, God with us. Thank You that You are with me and You are everything I need.

Mention your needs and then refer to any of the names of God that apply. For instance, "You are my Overcomer and I need to overcome my loneliness." Or "You are my Patience and I need patience today with _____."

I thank You that You are there for me in this way. Please help me sense Your presence in a new way today.

TOOLS OF TRUTH

They will call on My name,
And I will answer them.
I will say, "This is My people";
And each one will say, "The LORD is my God."

ZECHARIAH 13:9

Whoever calls on the name of the Lord shall be saved.

ROMANS 10:13

I will never fail you. I will never forsake you.

HEBREWS 13:5 NLT

Our help is in the name of the LORD.

PSALM 124:8

Therefore God also has highly exalted Him and given Him the name which is above every name.

PHILIPPIANS 2:9

Whoever acknowledges me before men, I will also acknowledge him before my Father in heaven.

MATTHEW 10:32 NIV

PART TWO

THE
SOLID
FOUNDATION

CHAPTER 8

PRAYING TO MOVE ON WITH THE LORD

I'm still on shaky ground," I said to myself as I drove to church one Sunday morning nearly a year after coming to know the Lord. Even though my life was much improved, I still had this uneasy feeling that at any moment I could lose the stability I'd gained. I feared that my glimpses of hope for the future would all come to nothing.

It was obvious that I had made *some* progress since that day in October with Terry and Pastor Jack. After all, in the beginning of my relationship with the Lord, I wasn't even able to get myself to church. For months Terry and her husband woke me on Sunday mornings with a phone call and then drove out of their way to pick me up, knowing I wasn't strong enough in my mind, body, or spirit to get there on my own. After they stopped taking me, my attendance was sporadic for a time until I resolved to get myself to church regularly *without* their assistance. Now as I was driving myself there for the fifth consecutive Sunday morning, I thought about what I had been learning.

I'd heard Pastor Jack preach every week about "moving on with the Lord," and it was finally starting to register. Each time he mentioned it, he waved his arm slowly across the congregation, like a shepherd trying to move his sheep in a certain direction. One morning as he waved his arm over the congregation, I realized that you don't just stay in one place after you receive the Lord. You have to start growing.

I thought that after you received Jesus into your life, that was it. You'd made it. No more problems. But I was finding that wasn't the case. The truth is, I *had* made it into eternity by securing life after death. However, my life here on earth still needed work. I had to do certain things daily to sustain life and become spiritually and emotionally healthy. What a revelation! Having pursued physical fitness and the concept of proper body care for many years, I quickly related to this discipline—doing something good for yourself, no matter how much you didn't *feel* like doing it, so that you would be able to enjoy good health and well-being. I began to understand that just as the physical body needs to be fed, exercised, and cleansed, so the spirit and soul need replenishing.

That morning in church I thought, *My foundation isn't as strong as it should be. That must be why I have times of doubt and feel like I'm on shaky ground. God, show me how to strengthen my relationship with You so that my foundation becomes solid.*

Over the next few months I learned about five key elements—spiritual building blocks—that will strengthen our relationship with God:

1. The Word of God
2. Prayer
3. Praise
4. Confession
5. Ongoing forgiveness

By neglecting even one of them, we end up with cracks in our foundation. When we have cracks in our foundation, we never end up where we are supposed to be and we can never fully know God's will.

Some people do "get by," never doing any of these things, but I wasn't interested in getting by. I'd been doing that for years. I wanted true spiritual well-being and a sense of purpose and direction. I wanted God's will for my life.

PRAYER

Lord, help me remember the importance of Your Word, prayer, praise, confession, and ongoing forgiveness in my daily walk. Help me not neglect any one of them. Open my mind and heart to walk even deeper with You in each of these areas.

TOOLS OF TRUTH

When the whirlwind passes by, the wicked is no more,
But the righteous has an everlasting foundation.

PROVERBS 10:25

Whoever hears these sayings of Mine, and does them, I will liken him to a wise man who built his house on the rock.

MATTHEW 7:24

Nevertheless the solid foundation of God stands, having this seal: "The Lord knows those who are His," and, "Let everyone who names the name of Christ depart from iniquity."

2 TIMOTHY 2:19

CHAPTER 9

PRAYING FOR A
SOLID FOUNDATION
IN GOD'S TRUTH

One morning as Pastor Jack once again encouraged us to "move on," this time in the Word of God, I thought, *First Pastor asks us to bring our own Bibles; now he wants us to read them ourselves?* I had purchased a Bible in a translation that I could understand, just as he had requested, but I thought that *he* would teach us from it and we would follow along.

I had given up trying to read the Bible years before when several unsuccessful attempts brought discouragement and frustration. I found the writing so foreign, I couldn't understand it at all. But Pastor Jack taught from the Scriptures with amazing clarity, and I hung on every word. It was like watching a movie so reflective of my own life that I became involved in the action.

Could it be, I asked myself, *that I might feel that same way when I read the Bible at home alone?*

The next morning I began reading in Psalms and Proverbs, which had short chapters and seemed to be safe enough for me to tackle. Over the following weeks I branched out into the gospels of Matthew, Mark, Luke, and John. I was surprised at the way every word came alive with new meaning. Soon I had such a desire to know the whole story that I started at the beginning of the Bible and read straight through to the end. When I finished months later, I felt as if I knew the heart of the Author and my life had been changed.

While I was reading semifaithfully each day, I noticed distinct and undeniable benefits. I discovered it was especially beneficial to read Scripture the first thing in the morning because it set my heart and mind on the right course for the day. Also reading the Bible before I went to bed at night ensured that I would sleep without nightmares, which had been a problem for as long as I could remember.

Gradually the Bible became God's voice in my ear. When I heard certain old, familiar words in my mind, such as *You're worthless. You'll never amount to anything. Why try?* I also heard the words of God saying, *You are fearfully and wonderfully made. I will lift you up from the gates of death. You will be blessed if you put your trust in Me* (Pss. 139:14; 9:13; 2:12).

The more I read, the more I saw that God's laws were good. They were there for my benefit, and I could trust them. It became clear to me that conscience wasn't an adequate indicator of right or wrong. I could see that things can really only be found right or wrong in the light of God's Word. Such guidelines, rather than restricting, were actually liberating to me.

Even when His Word did not specifically say, "This is right" or "This is wrong," my spirit became so aligned with His that I could sense what was correct. For example, while the Bible *did* say not to be drunk, I no longer felt it was even a good idea for me to drink alcohol for a "relaxed" feeling, especially in light of my history of alcohol and drug abuse. Besides, the "high" I was getting from being in the presence of the Lord was far greater than any I could derive from other sources. This was just one of many beginning signs of emotional maturity and wholeness that were being worked in my soul, the foundation of which was laid in the Word of God.

WHAT? ME, READ?

You may be thinking, *I can't afford the time it takes to read the Bible every day.* Let me challenge you to reconsider. On page 66 I have listed fifteen reasons to read the Bible daily. After you read this list you will realize that we can't afford to let a day go by without absorbing at least a few verses of the Word into our hearts and minds.

Good relationships, good health, and being good at what you do all require some sacrifice, discipline, discomfort, and

FIFTEEN REASONS TO READ THE BIBLE DAILY

1. To be rid of anxiety and have peace (Ps. 119:165)

2. To set things right when life is out of control (Ps. 19:7–8)

3. To have direction and know God's will (Ps. 119:105)

4. To experience healing and deliverance (Ps. 107:20)

5. To grow in the Lord (1 Peter 2:2)

6. To have strength, comfort, and hope (Ps. 119:28, 50, 114)

7. To shape yourself and your life correctly (Ps. 119:11)

8. To be able to see clearly (Ps. 119:130)

9. To know what's really in your heart (Heb. 4:12)

10. To build faith (Rom. 10:17)

11. To have joy (Ps. 16:11)

12. To understand God's power (John 1:3)

13. To have more life in this life (Ps. 119:50)

14. To distinguish good from evil (Ps. 119:101–2)

15. To understand God's love for you (John 1:14)

even some pain. Spiritual wholeness is like that too. Reading God's Word must become a daily discipline because we need a solid grasp of the way God intends us to live if we are going to live for Him. The Bible says, "Man shall not live by bread alone, but by every word that proceeds from the mouth of God" (Matt. 4:4). Regular feeding on God's Word satisfies the hunger of our souls and keeps us from emotional depletion and spiritual starvation. It also keeps us in the center of God's will.

Perhaps you wonder as I did at one point, *How can I be sure that the Bible is really God's Word?* I reply to that question by asking another: "How can you be sure it isn't?" The only way you can know about a book for certain is to read it straight through. You can't judge the Author unless you've read His book.

Don't let *other* people tell you what God's Word says (even if they are great Bible teachers like Pastor Jack); read it for yourself, keeping in mind that it was written for *you*. Get up early to read the Bible in the morning, if at all possible, in order to set the tone for the day. If you can't read then, decide when you can. Midmorning? Lunch hour? After dinner? Before bed? Make this an appointment with God and write it down on your calendar.

If the version of the Bible you're reading is difficult to understand, get another translation. I have used the New King James, the New International Version, and the New Living Translation in this book; other versions, such as the New American Standard or the Amplified Bible, are also easy to read. If you can't afford to buy a more readable translation, ask around for one. Make a bold request of your pastor. There are people all over the world who would like nothing better than to give you a Bible if you just let them know your needs.

WHAT IF I'M HURTING?

At times in my battle with fear and depression, I sat down to read the Word of God feeling so depleted, numb, or pre-occupied, I could hardly even comprehend the words. I not only didn't feel close to God but felt it futile to hope He could ever change me or my life in any lasting way. In spite of that, as I read I was struck by a remarkable lifting of those negative emotions. Afterward I may not have been able to pass a quiz on the passage, but I felt renewed, strengthened, and hopeful.

When you feel fearful, depressed, or anxious, take the Bible in hand and say, "My soul is starving, and this is food for my spirit. I want to do the right thing, and reading the Bible is always the right thing to do." Pray the prayer at the end of this chapter, and then begin to read God's Word until you sense peace coming into your heart.

While the Bible was written to give you knowledge of the Lord, it takes the Holy Spirit to bring a particular Scripture alive to your heart. When that happens, take it as God speaking words of comfort, hope, and guidance directly to you. The Bible says, "For whatever things were written before were written for our learning, that we through the patience and comfort of the Scriptures might have hope" (Rom. 15:4).

BUT I ALREADY KNOW THAT!

Don't say, "I've already read the Bible. I've memorized a hundred scriptures, and I even teach Bible classes, so I don't need to read it every day." This is dangerous thinking. Whenever you eat food or drink water, you don't say, "I won't have to do that again," do you? Of course not. Your body needs to be fed daily. The same goes for your spiritual and emotional self. And because you're not the same person today as you were the day before, every time you read God's Word, you will receive it in a new and different way. In fact, if you've read your Bible many, many times, buy a *new* Bible in a different translation or the same translation in a different form, and read through it again. You'll be surprised how new and fresh the Word is to you.

Some groups of people reject God's Word by setting for themselves a lifestyle that opposes God's design for their lives. They believe they know it all and don't need His truth. However, if you watch long enough, you'll eventually see them destroy themselves. This lifestyle may appear to be working for a time, but don't be deceived into thinking it always will. Anyone who rejects God's truth will wind up the loser. We also lose part of our protective armor when we know God's truth but don't allow it regular opportunity to penetrate our lives in new and fresh ways.

It helps to keep in mind that the Bible is God's love letter to you. When you receive letters from someone you love, you don't just read them once and never look at them again. You pore over them time after time, drinking in the very essence of that person, looking between the lines for any and every possible message. God's love letters to you are full of messages. They say, "This is how much I love you." They do *not* say, "These are the things you need to do to *get* Me to love you." The Bible is not just a collection of information; it is a book of life. It's not to be read as a ritual or out of fear that something bad will happen if you don't. It's to be read so that God can build you up in His love from the inside out and brand His nature into your heart so that nothing can keep you away from His presence or out of His will.

PRAYER

Lord, I thank You for Your Word. Reveal Yourself to me as I read it and let it come alive in my heart and mind. Show me what I need to know. Let Your Word penetrate anything that would block me from receiving all You want to say to me today.

TOOLS OF TRUTH

If you abide in Me, and My words abide in you, you will ask
what you desire, and it shall be done for you.

JOHN 15:7

For the word of God is living and powerful, and sharper
than any two-edged sword, piercing even to the division of
soul and spirit, and of joints and marrow, and is a discerner
of the thoughts and intents of the heart.

HEBREWS 4:12

He sent His word and healed them,
And delivered them from their destructions.

PSALM 107:20

The testimony of the LORD is sure, making wise the simple;
The statutes of the LORD are right, rejoicing the heart;
The commandment of the LORD is pure, enlightening the eyes.

PSALM 19:7–8

The grass withers, the flower fades,
But the word of our God stands forever.

ISAIAH 40:8

CHAPTER 10

PRAYING TO KNOW
THE POWER
OF PRAYER

During the first couple of years I walked with the Lord, my prayers went something like this:

- "God, help me get that job."
- "Jesus, please heal my throat."
- "Lord, send enough money to pay these bills."
- "Father, take away my fear."

It took me a while to realize that those spur-of-the-moment prayers were not accomplishing much. I thought I should do the best I could on my own, and then if I needed a lifeline from God, I could grab for it. The only problem was, I needed a lifeline every other minute.

I loved the Scripture that says, "Ask, and it will be given to you; seek, and you will find; knock, and it will be opened to you" (Matt. 7:7). I took God at His word and was asking, seeking, and knocking on a pray-as-you-go basis. I also took to heart the Scripture that says, "You do not have because you do not ask" (James 4:2). *Great! I can easily remedy that,* I thought, and I proceeded to ask for everything. But I was still not happy, and I didn't see the kind of answered prayer I desired.

One day as I was again reading that same verse, my eyes were opened to the next verse: "You ask and do not receive, because you ask amiss, that you may spend it on your pleasures" (James 4:3). Could it be that the "God-give-me-this, do-that, wave-Your-magic-wand-here, get-me-out-of-this-mess" kind of praying was not what God desired for my prayer life? In utter frustration I said, "Lord, teach me how I'm supposed to pray."

He did exactly that!

I came to understand that prayer is not just asking for things—although that certainly is part of it. Far more important, prayer is talking with God. It's getting close to and spending time with the One you love. It's seeking Him first, touching Him, getting to know Him better, being with Him, and waiting in His presence. It's acknowledging Him as the source of power upon whom you depend. It's taking the time to say, *Speak to my heart, Lord, and tell me what I need to hear.*

Still later I came across the Scripture that says, "For your

Father knows the things you have need of before you ask Him" (Matt. 6:8). This puzzled me, so I questioned Pastor Jack: "If God already knows what I need, why do I even need to ask for anything?"

In his usual clear manner, he explained, "Because God has given us a free will. He has set it up so that we always have a choice about everything we do, including whether or not we choose to communicate with Him. He will never intervene where man does not want Him."

Of course! I thought. *God wants us to desire to be with Him. There is no love relationship if one person has to dictate how the other must think, feel, and act.*

"God *knows* our thoughts," Pastor Jack continued, "but He *responds* to our prayers. We have to come to a place of realizing that prayer is a *privilege* that is always *ours*, but the *power* in prayer is always *His. Without God, we can't do it. Without us, God won't do it.*"

That put a whole new perspective on the subject. Things wouldn't happen in my life unless I prayed. And I was no longer just asking for things; I was partnering with God. I was aligning my spirit with His, and together we would see that *His* perfect will would be done.

One significant example of this was my prayer for a husband. I had been married before I became a believer, but after the failure of that marriage, I seriously doubted I could ever be happily married. It was what I wanted most, but it wasn't until I started praying about it that I began to have hope.

Lord, is there someone with whom I can share my life? I

prayed, *Someone I can love without being rejected? Someone who loves You and me and will be faithful to both of us?*

I had only been praying that prayer a short time when I started dating Michael Omartian, and I was desperately afraid of making another mistake. But God had taught me how to pray about such matters, so that's what I did.

"Lord, I thank You for Michael," I prayed every day, "but if he is not the husband You have for me, take him out of my life. Close the door on our relationship. I don't want to live my way anymore. I want *Your* will to be done in my life. I seek You first, knowing You will provide all that I need."

The more I prayed that prayer, the closer Michael and I became until finally we were both certain we were to be together. In the twenty-eight years we've been married, neither of us has wondered if we married the wrong person, even during the toughest times. That's because our relationship was covered and committed to God in prayer from the beginning. And we know that prayer has held us together. Being able to come into God's presence with our hearts open to being changed kept us growing together instead of falling apart. As I said in my book *The Power of a Praying Wife*, prayer and our commitment to doing things God's way have kept us out of divorce court when our flesh might have welcomed it in weak moments.

From an issue as major as marrying the right person to something as minor as preparing a meal for dinner guests, everything I did was covered in prayer. Little by little the fabric of my life began to change, and wholeness crept into it the way damaged cells repair themselves in response to a healing ointment.

HOW TO PRAY EFFECTIVELY

We all know that when friends don't see each other and communicate frequently, they can become emotionally separated. Well, it's the same with you and God. If you don't keep in touch with Him, you begin to feel distant from Him even when you're not. This is why you must pray daily. Also, when you spend time with someone you respect, the character of that person rubs off on you. When you are in the presence of God, His character is formed *in* you.

Many of us are especially vulnerable to the enemy's attack on our self-worth. It doesn't take much to discourage us, and feeling distant from God will do it. That's why it's important to start the day with some kind of prayer. We have to establish ourselves and our lives as being connected to Him.

We can't receive God's best for our lives, and we can't push back the things that were never God's will for us, except through prayer. We have to learn that we can't leave our lives to chance. We have to pray over anything that concerns us, no matter how big—"With God nothing will be impossible" (Luke 1:37)—or how small—"The very hairs of your head are all numbered" (Matt. 10:30).

If you have any doubt about the importance of prayer or if you are still praying on an on-again/off-again basis, go through the fifteen reasons to pray below. I find that reading the Scripture passages that support them is very motivational too.

FIFTEEN REASONS TO PRAY

1. To seek the face of the Lord and know Him better (Ps. 27:8)
2. To get your eyes off your problems and onto the Lord (Ps. 121:1)
3. To speak to God (1 Peter 3:12)
4. To unburden your heart (Ps. 142:1–2)
5. To make your requests known to God (Matt. 21:22)
6. To hear God (Prov. 8:34)
7. To be free of suffering (James 5:13)
8. To resist temptation (Matt. 26:41)
9. To be rescued from distress (Ps. 107:19)
10. To receive God's reward (Matt. 6:6)
11. To withstand evil (Eph. 6:13)
12. To have joy (John 16:24)
13. To get close to God (Isa. 64:7)
14. To be healed emotionally (James 5:13)
15. To have peace (Phil. 4:6–7)

Do whatever you have to do to secure a place and time to pray. When I was single and during the first few years of marriage, that was not a problem. However, after our first child was born it was much more difficult. When our second child arrived, the only way I could spend time with the Lord was to get up at 5:30 A.M. The only place I could go at that hour and not disturb anyone was a small walk-in closet off the master bath. What a contrast to my early years of being locked in the closet for punishment! Now I went there to commune with God. This went well for a while until I was discovered. First I was visited regularly by my eighteen-month-old daughter, who learned to climb out of her crib and come looking for me. Soon she was followed by her six-year-old brother.

One morning, when both of them, plus my husband, two dogs, and several hamsters, ended up in the closet, I knew it was time to either get up earlier or find a new location. Sometimes we have to revise our plans, but securing a time and place to be alone with God is worth any effort.

Without reducing prayer to a formula, I found that it is good to include certain key points in each prayer time:

- Tell the Lord how much you love Him.

- Thank Him for all He has done for you.

- State how dependent you are upon Him.

- Tell Him everything that's in your heart.

- Confess anything that needs to be confessed.

- Give Him all your requests.

- Wait for Him to speak to your heart.

- Praise Him for working powerfully in your life.

Don't ever feel inhibited because you think you can't pray. If you can talk, you can pray. And don't be concerned about prayer talk, church talk, or Christianese talk. The Bible tells us the only qualifications we need: "He who comes to God must believe that He is, and that He is a rewarder of those who diligently seek Him" (Heb. 11:6). We just have to believe that He is a good God.

The more you pray, the more you will find to pray about, and the more you'll be led to pray for others: family members (as in my books *The Power of a Praying Wife* and *The Power of a Praying Parent*), friends, enemies, and all those in authority in any area of your life (pastor, teacher, boss, governor, president). You'll pray for them not only because they influence your emotional health and because part of the peace you experience will result directly from that type of praying, but because Jesus asked you to do it.

DOES GOD ALWAYS HEAR MY PRAYERS?

You can never be disqualified as a person of prayer, so don't be discouraged by negative voices like, *You're not good enough to come before God's throne*, or *You've failed again, so don't go crying back to God.* Lies, lies, lies! Don't listen to any of them. Picture a Father who never works late, never ignores or rejects you, is never too busy, and is always waiting for you to come and talk with Him. And even though you have many brothers and sisters, you are never in competition with them because He has no favorites. I know that kind of love is hard to receive if you've never been loved like that as a child, but that's your heavenly Father's availability for you. As Pastor Jack Hayford so succinctly puts it, "Your heavenly Father is waiting to hear from you. Call home!"

Don't allow discouragement over unanswered prayer to cause you to doubt that God has heard you. If you have received Jesus and are praying in His name, then God hears you, and something is happening whether you see it manifested in your life now or not. In fact, every time you pray, you're advancing God's purposes for you. Without prayer, the full purpose God has for you can't happen.

POWER IN NUMBERS

It's important to understand that spiritual well-being depends upon two kinds of regular prayer. One is deep, intimate prayer alone—just you and God. The other is prayer together with other believers—praying for one another. The battle to confront temptation and stay in the center of God's will becomes far too difficult to fight entirely alone. We need others praying with us to give us strength, to help us think straight, to lift our vision above our circumstances.

The Bible says, "Where two or three are gathered together in My name, I am there in the midst of them" (Matt. 18:20). There is power in two or more people praying together because God's presence attends it. This is one of His promises, and when He promises something, He doesn't *try* to keep His promises, as you and I do; He *does* keep them. I don't believe you can find complete spiritual well-being unless people are standing with you in prayer.

My friend Diane, whom I led to the Lord, had been my best friend since high school. Because we had similar dysfunctional family situations, we understood each other's prayer needs and fell into the habit of praying regularly together over the phone several times a week. It was actually easier to pray for *her* than it was to pray for myself, because there was no end to the possibilities I could see for her. (I have found that you can pray only so much for yourself without getting bored or frustrated because of being too close to your own situation.) Our prayers for one another were instrumental in our spiritual growth.

Gradually my prayer partners increased from one to three, then five, and eventually seven. These groups met in my home every week for years. My husband, Michael, and I also had a number of couples meet with us to pray on a monthly basis. With that many people united in prayer for one another, someone is praying for each member all the time. I can't imagine facing life without that support.

When my family and I moved to another state, we had to start all over again because we didn't know many people.

But we were blessed in that my sister, Suzy, and her family and my close friend, Roz, and her family moved to the same town at the same time. They had been part of my prayer group for years. This was not a coincidence. I believe God was in the center of their decision, just as He was in the center of ours.

Right away, Suzy, Roz, and I started our prayer group with just the three of us. At first I thought, *Lord, will our prayers be powerful enough with only three people praying? Yet I know You say that when two or three are gathered together in Your name, You will be in the midst of them. We need You desperately to be in our midst every day.*

In those early days we prayed for God to send new members to our prayer group. We prayed for our church. Our neighborhoods. Our community. If one of us was sick, the other two would be there in prayer. If one of us was weak, the other two would hold her up in prayer. We were grateful for the strength of one another's prayers, and we became more and more dependent on God for every step we took. We each agreed that we didn't know how we could survive that difficult transition without those prayers.

Everyone needs one or more persons with whom they can pray and agree every month, every week, or every day if need be. You need that too. This must go two ways, though. *You* must be praying for *them*, also. Don't be afraid, shy, or hesitant to take this crucial step. Ask God to lead you to at least one other believer, and be bold enough to ask that person if he or she wants to pray with you regularly. If the first person you ask can't do it or it doesn't work out, don't feel rejected or get discouraged; just keep looking for the right one. And don't hesitate to pray for someone's requests because you fear your prayers won't be answered, as I did in the beginning. *Remember, your job is to do the praying; it's God's job to answer the prayers.*

If you are blessed enough to have a husband who will pray with you regularly, that's excellent. However, if your spouse seems less than enthusiastic about the idea, don't fret, badger, or nag. We can never dictate how other people are supposed to act, *especially* husbands. Just let it go. Your spiritual well-being and happiness doesn't depend on him. It depends on God. Don't allow disappointment in your spouse's spirituality deter you. This is the enemy's trap to cause strife in the home and keep you from moving into all the Lord has for you.

Whether you pray with others or you pray alone, it's beneficial to read the Word of God *before* you pray because it prepares your heart to pray according to God's will. Have a pencil and paper with you so you can write down anything the Lord speaks to your heart. If you need an ability to pray beyond your own capabilities because you are too weak, too upset, or too frightened, ask the Holy Spirit to help you.

Once you pray about something, put it in God's hands. That doesn't mean you don't pray about it again; it just means that you have laid that burden at the Lord's feet. The answer will *always* come, although it might not be in the way you expect or according to your timing. Most important, you have spent time in the Lord's presence, where you can hear God speak to you about His will for your life.

PRAYER

Lord, I have a deep desire to draw close to You in prayer. Help me rise above the distractions and busyness that rob me of those times with You. Help me make prayer a priority so that I can learn what Your will is for my life.

TOOLS OF TRUTH

The effective, fervent prayer of a righteous man avails much.

JAMES 5:16

And whatever things you ask in prayer, believing, you will receive.

MATTHEW 21:22

I cry out to the LORD with my voice;
. . . .
I pour out my complaint before Him;
I declare before Him my trouble.

PSALM 142:1–2

Is anyone among you suffering? Let him pray.

JAMES 5:13

For the eyes of the LORD are on the righteous,
And His ears are open to their prayers.

1 PETER 3:12

CHAPTER 11

PRAYING TO UNDERSTAND THE FREEDOM IN PRAISE

I can't do it!" I cried to God in prayer shortly after Michael and I were married. "I can't handle the dishes. I can't handle the house. I can't handle my work. I can't handle the loneliness of being a wife of someone who works all the time. I can't deal with my own emotional ups and downs, let alone my husband's! I can't do any of it, God, not any of it!" I wept before the Lord with a mixture of frustration and guilt over the fact that I was feeling this way about my husband, my home, and my life. God had rescued me and given me hope and a future. How could I—who knew what it was to be hungry and poor and feel that there was no love or purpose in my life—tell God I couldn't handle these answers to my own prayers?

Fortunately, the Lord did not strike me with lightning; instead He waited quietly until I was finished and then softly reminded me, *You are trying to do everything in your own strength.* As I sat there in my discouragement, I sensed the Holy Spirit speaking to my heart, saying simply, *All you have to do is worship Me in the midst of what you are facing, and I will do the rest.*

"Oh, thank You, Lord," I prayed through my tears. "I think I can at least handle doing that much."

I lifted my hands and said out loud, "Lord, I praise You in the midst of my situation. Thank You that You are all-powerful and there is nothing too hard for You. Thank You for who You are and all You have done for me. I worship You, Jesus, Almighty God, Holy Father, Lord of my life.

"Lord, I give You my home, my marriage, my husband, and my work. They are Yours," I said as my shoulders relaxed, the knot in my stomach left, and I sighed with tears of relief. The pressure was off. I felt free of the burden I had been carrying, because the burden was now *His.* I didn't have to try to be perfect anymore, and I didn't have to beat myself up when I wasn't all I thought I should be.

Since that time, praise has become a habitual attitude of my heart that says, "No matter what is going on in and around me, *God is in charge!* I trust Him to bring good out of this situation and work things out for my highest blessing."

Praise is not always my first reaction to things, however, so I often have to remind myself of Pastor Jack Hayford's teaching on praise. He said, "It's not your saying, 'I'll give it everything I've got and the Lord will bless it,' but rather it's the Lord saying to you, 'You just bless My name and *I'll* give it everything *I* have.'"

Now, when I come to the place where my flesh can't go

any further, I stop where I am and worship God. This key has unlocked even the heaviest of closet doors and illuminated the darkest of nights. It frees you to get your mind off yourself and onto the Lord. It helps you find your way when you don't know the next step to take.

A KEY TO TRANSFORMATION

Worship is powerful because God's presence comes to dwell in our midst when we praise Him, and in His presence we find healing, transformation, and direction for our lives. In fact, the more time we spend praising the Lord, the more we will see ourselves and our circumstances grow in wholeness and completeness. That's because praise softens our hearts and makes them pliable. It also covers us protectively. The more the pliability and covering are maintained, the more quickly our hearts can be molded and healed.

Please read the preceding paragraph again. Underline it, circle it, draw arrows pointing to it, commit it to memory, write it on your hand, or do whatever you have to do to remember it. This important truth is the first thing we forget and the last thing we remember because our flesh doesn't naturally want to do it.

Praise and worship of God are always acts of will. Sometimes our problems or the burdens we carry choke out our good intentions, so we have to make the effort to establish praise as a way of life. And it becomes a way of life when we make it our *first* reaction to what we face and not a last resort. That's when we find true freedom in the Lord.

Now is the time to start being thankful to God for everything in your life. Thank Him for His Word, His faithfulness, His love, His grace, His healing. Thank Him for what He has done for you personally. If you have trouble thinking of something, then thank Him that you're still breathing and that you can read. Keep in mind that whatever you thank the Lord for—peace, financial blessing, health, a new job, an end to depression—will start the process of its being released to you at that time. Read the list of "Fifteen Reasons to Praise the Lord" on page 91 to help motivate you. There has to be at least one that will make you want to praise God.

In the Old Testament, the people who carried the Ark of the Covenant stopped every six steps to worship. We, too, need to remind ourselves not to go very far without stopping to worship. For spiritual well-being, we have to be six-step persons and continually invite the presence of the Lord to rule in our situations. We have to be free to praise Him no matter what our circumstances.

The reason people don't give thanks to God in praise is because they don't know Him well enough. The more you know of Him, the more you perceive His goodness, the more you can't help but thank, praise, and worship Him for who He is and what He has done. And the more you do that, the more joy you will have in your heart. Pastor Jack Hayford describes joy as "that inner, happy confidence that there is nothing that can successfully resist the inevitability of Christ's certain triumph in me." What a wonderful thing to know about yourself. Such knowledge of the Lord is the foundation for your spiritual well-being and the foundational step in understanding God's will for your life.

FIFTEEN REASONS TO PRAISE THE LORD

1. To enthrone God and acknowledge His greatness (Ps. 95:1–5)

2. To increase our awareness of God's presence (Ps. 103)

3. To have the joy of the Lord (Ps. 30)

4. To acknowledge God's hand in every area of our lives (Ps. 91)

5. To release God's power into our situations (Ps. 144)

6. To know God better (Ps. 50:23)

7. To break our chains of bondage and bring deliverance (Ps. 50:14–15)

8. To be under God's covering of safety and protection (Ps. 95:6–7)

9. To strengthen the soul and be transformed (Ps. 138:1–3)

10. To receive guidance and establish God's purposes in our lives (Ps. 16:7–11)

11. To thwart the devil's plans for our destruction (Ps. 92)

12. To dissipate doubt and increase faith (Ps. 27)

13. To be delivered from fear (Ps. 34)

14. To bring a fresh flow of His Holy Spirit in us (Ps. 40)

15. To possess all that God has promised for us (Ps. 147)

WORSHIP, GOD'S WAY

To have spiritual well-being and to know God's will, we must worship God *His* way. However, *His* way often doesn't fit our schedule or style. There are several ways to praise God that don't always come easily but are crucial to spiritual health. Freedom in praise brings a powerful release.

1. *Praise is meant to be sung.* King David says in Psalm 147:1, "It is good to sing praises to our God; for it is pleasant, and praise is beautiful." This is often hard for us because at times singing is the last thing we feel like doing, or we're so self-conscious about our voices that we don't open our mouths, even when we're alone. Yet in the Bible the singers went before the troops into battle because their singing praise to God confused the enemy. It works exactly the same way for us today.

Many times in the early days of my walk with God, my soul was tormented with such depression in the middle of the night that I would get up, shut myself in my prayer closet so I wouldn't wake anyone, and sing softly to the Lord. I'd sing a hymn, or a chorus, or make up a song. Sometimes all I could sing was "Thank You, Jesus. Praise You, Lord," over and over until I felt the oppression leave and strength and life come into my soul.

You may be so depressed or hurting that you feel you can't even unclench your jaw. When that happens say, "God, give me a song in my heart that I can sing to You," and begin to hum to the Lord any melody that comes to mind. Then put words to it that are from your heart. Don't worry about the pitch, the rhythm, the melody, or the sound of your voice. Sing it all on one note if you want. Remember, the true singer is the one who has God's song in his heart. The Lord thinks your voice is beautiful. He designed it for the purpose of praising Him. Continue to sing over your situation because, as you do, something is happening in the spirit realm and you will feel the heaviness lift.

2. *Praise is meant to be expressed with the lifting of your hands:* "Lift up your hands in the sanctuary, and bless the LORD" (Ps. 134:2). Lifting our hands to the Lord as we praise God is also an act of the will that is not second nature to us. It is really not the strength of our arms that lifts our hands, but rather it is the heart. When our hearts are full of thanks to God, it's far easier to lift up our hands and praise Him. However, when our hearts are heavy, sad, depressed, angry, discouraged, or tired, we still must make ourselves lift them up. Worship is the exercise of spirit overcoming our flesh. We have to say to ourselves, "I *will* rejoice and be glad. I *will* lift my hands to the Lord." We can't wait for good feelings first. We have to lift our hands and let go of ourselves so the joy of the Lord can rise in our hearts.

The most important reason for you to do this is to let go of everything you're holding on to and surrender to God: "I give up, Lord." You can also think of it as taking your life in your hands and offering it up to Him: "I give You everything of myself, Lord."

The more you lift up to God in submission, the more

freedom you will know. Remember, everything God asks you to do is for *your* benefit, not His. He doesn't ask you to do things that will embarrass you or make you feel stupid. He asks you to do things that will make you more whole and give your life greater meaning.

3. *Praise is meant to be done together with others as well as alone.* "In the midst of the assembly I will sing praise to You" (Heb. 2:12). I used to hurry into the church thirty minutes late on Sunday mornings. By the time I found a seat and settled into it, the worship time was over and the pastor was preaching. I wasn't concerned about this because I was there for the teaching. Yet my mind wandered everywhere and didn't settle into the message until the sermon was half over.

On the days I arrived in plenty of time to get a seat *before* the service started and was a full participant through the entire worship time, I found I was open to receive the message as if God was speaking directly to me. My heart was made soft and receptive to what the Holy Spirit wanted to teach me because of the thirty to forty minutes I had spent worshiping God in unity with other believers. Negative attitudes I had come in with were melted away and replaced with ones more in alignment with what God desired.

Don't miss times of worship with other believers. Corporate worship is powerful to the point of breaking down strongholds in your life and allowing changes that might not take place otherwise. Many negative emotions will be released from your heart in group worship, and this will protect you from all that steals your peace.

A WEAPON AGAINST FUTILITY

Without praise we experience an eroding that leads to bondage and death. The Bible says, "Although they knew God, they did not glorify Him as God, nor were thankful, but became *futile* in their *thoughts*, and their foolish *hearts* were *darkened*" (Rom. 1:21, emphasis added). With praise you and your circumstances can be changed, because it gives God entrance into every area of your life and allows Him to be enthroned there.

So any time you struggle with negative emotions, such as anger, unforgiveness, fear, hurt, depression, or worthlessness, thank God that He is bigger than all that. Thank Him that His plans and purposes for you are good. Thank Him that in any weak area of your life, He will be strong. Thank Him that He came to restore you. Remember the names of the Lord, and use them in your worship. "I praise You, Lord, because You are my Deliverer and Redeemer." "Thank You, God, that You are my Healer and Provider." Once you align yourself with God's purposes through praise, you can thank Him for things that you can't see yet in your life as though they were there.

For instance, if you are angry with a spouse or friend, you might pray, "Lord, I don't seem to be able to get over my anger at this person, but You are all-powerful and can make it happen. I thank You and praise You for Your power in my life." Doing this is your greatest weapon against the feelings of anger or inadequacy that undermine all God has made you to be.

PRAYER

Lord, I thank You that You are my strength. Thank You that no matter what I face at this moment, You are greater. I am grateful that You give me the knowledge and strength I need to get where I need to go. I praise You this day for who You are and for Your goodness to me.

TOOLS OF TRUTH

Let us continually offer the sacrifice of praise to God, that is, the fruit of our lips, giving thanks to His name.

HEBREWS 13:15

But the hour is coming, and now is, when the true worshipers will worship the Father in spirit and truth; for the Father is seeking such to worship Him.

JOHN 4:23

Rejoice always . . . in everything give thanks; for this is the will of God in Christ Jesus for you.

1 THESSALONIANS 5:16, 18

I will render praises to You,
For You have delivered my soul from death.

PSALM 56:12–13

But you are . . . His own special people, that you may proclaim the praises of Him who called you out of darkness into His marvelous light.

1 PETER 2:9

CHAPTER 12

PRAYING FOR RELEASE FROM UNCONFESSED SIN

Unconfessed sin affects our whole life. And often we don't recognize it.

After I came to know the Lord and experienced that warm, close, rich feeling of walking with God, I still fell back into some old, familiar bad habits. I had only known the Lord for a few months before I went out on tour with a music group. None of them were believers, and so it was easy to be drawn back into their drinking and partying lifestyle.

When I came home after a month of that decadent life, I went back to church but I didn't feel the intimacy with God that I had been experiencing before I left. I recognized that it was probably because God was not pleased with the way I had been living the past four weeks. I began to feel guilty, depressed, and hopeless about my life again.

PRAYING GOD'S WILL FOR YOUR LIFE

The following Sunday, Pastor Jack talked about the damage unconfessed sin can do to your soul. I knew that God was talking to me. Right there in church I quietly confessed to the Lord my sinful actions of the past month. The moment I did, I felt that wonderful sense of God's love again, and I couldn't stop the tears from flowing. Here I had been thinking that God had turned His back on me, but the truth was that my actions had separated me from Him. I hated that feeling of being distant from God, and I vowed to never let unconfessed sin come between me and the Lord again. I would try my best to live His way, but if I failed, I would confess it immediately so I could receive His forgiveness and not lose the close fellowship with Him that I had come to treasure so dearly.

THE WEIGHT OF UNCONFESSED SIN

When sin is unconfessed, it becomes a subtle growth, wrapping its tentacles around every part of our beings until we are paralyzed. The agony of it is accurately described in the Bible by King David:

> When I kept silent, my bones grew old
> Through my groaning all the day long.
> For day and night Your hand was heavy upon me;
> My vitality was turned into the drought of summer.
> I acknowledged my sin to You,
> And my iniquity I have not hidden.

I said, "I will confess my transgressions to the LORD,"
And You forgave the iniquity of my sin. (Ps. 32:3–5)

When sin is left unconfessed, a wall goes up between you and God. Even though the sin may have stopped, if it hasn't been confessed before the Lord, it will still weigh you down, dragging you back toward the past you are trying to leave behind and keeping you from moving into the future God has for you. I know because I used to carry around a bag of failures on my back that was so heavy I could barely move. I didn't realize how spiritually stooped over I had become. When I confessed my sins, I actually felt the weight being lifted.

Many of us suffer from low self-esteem, fear, and guilt. We mentally beat up on ourselves, tend to think the worst about our situations, and feel responsible for everything that goes wrong. It's true we can have times of feeling guilty for things we have done, but we don't have to be tortured by living endlessly in guilt. God provided the key of confession to release us from that.

Often we fail to see ourselves as responsible for certain actions. For example, while it's not your fault that someone hurt you, your *reaction* to it is your responsibility. You may feel justified in your anger or bitterness, but you still must confess it because it misses the mark of what God has for you. If you don't, its weight will eventually crush you. It will get you off the path God has for you.

THE KEY IS REPENTANCE

For confession to work, repentance must go along with it. Repentance literally means a change of mind. It means to turn your back, walk away, and decide not to do it again. It means getting your thinking aligned correctly with God. It's possible to confess without ever really conceding any fault at all. In fact, we can become simply good apologizers with no intent of being any other way. Confession and repentance mean saying, "This is my fault. I'm sorry about it, and I'm not going to do it anymore."

All sin has to be confessed and repented of for you to be free of bondage, whether you feel bad about it or not and whether you recognize it as sin or not. The Bible says, "My conscience is clear, but that does not make me innocent" (1 Cor. 4:4 NIV).

Every time you confess something, check to see if you honestly and truly do not want to do that anymore. And remember, God "knows the secrets of the heart" (Ps. 44:21). Being repentant doesn't necessarily mean you will never do it again, but it does mean you don't *intend* to do it again. If you find that you are committing the same sin over and over, you need to confess it each time. If you have committed a sin that you just confessed the day before, don't let that come between you and God. Confess it again. As long as you are truly repentant each time, you will be forgiven and eventually you will be completely set free. The Bible says, "Repent therefore and be converted, that your sins may be blotted out, so that times of refreshing may come from the presence of the Lord" (Acts 3:19).

Because we are not perfect, confession and repentance are ongoing. There are always new levels of Jesus' life that need to be worked in us. We fall short of the glory of God in ways that we can't yet even imagine. Therefore we need to also confess our hidden faults.

CONFESSING HIDDEN FAULTS

When you are building a foundation, you have to dig out the dirt. The trouble is, most of us don't go deep enough. While you can't see all your errors all the time, you *can* have a heart that is willing to be taught by the Lord. Ask God to bring to light sins you are not aware of so that they can be confessed, repented of, and forgiven. Recognize that there is something to confess every day and pray frequently as David did:

See if there is any wicked way in me,
And lead me in the way everlasting. (Ps. 139:24)

Create in me a clean heart, O God,
And renew a steadfast spirit within me. (Ps. 51:10)

Cleanse me from secret faults. (Ps. 19:12)

Sometimes when we don't think we have anything to confess, praying for God's revelation will reveal an unrepentant

103

attitude, such as criticism or unforgiveness, that has taken root in the heart. Confessing it keeps us from having to pay the emotional, spiritual, and physical price for it. It will also benefit our social lives since the imperfections in our personalities, which we can't see, are often obvious to others.

Sin leads to death; repentance leads to life. The amount of time that passes between the sin and the repentance will account for how much death is reaped in our lives. If we've reaped a lot of death, the problems won't go away immediately when we confess. But our confession has started the process of reversing what has taken place as a result of the sin.

There is also much healing when we confess our faults to another person for the purpose of prayer. The Bible says, "Confess your trespasses to one another, and pray for one another, that you may be healed" (James 5:16). Ask the Lord to show you when it is right to do that. But choose a person to confess to who is trustworthy and won't use the information against you.

Always keep in mind that God's ways are for your benefit. Confession is not for Him to find out something; He already knows. Confession is for *you* to be made whole. He is not standing over you, waiting to punish you for what you do wrong. He doesn't have to, because the punishment is inherent in the sin. People who confess find mercy and God's unlimited power.

PRAYER

Dear Lord, I know that I have sinned in this way:
_____. *Forgive me for my error. It grieves me to stumble like this, and I vow to turn my back on this sin. I'm not only sorry; I am truly repentant. Help me overcome any tendency toward this in my life.*

I also ask You to cleanse me from secret faults. Show me where I don't live Your way and help me correct these errors.

Lord, I don't want to miss all You have for me. I don't want to cover my sins and not prosper. I want to forsake them and live in Your mercy.

TOOLS OF TRUTH

He who covers his sins will not prosper,
But whoever confesses and forsakes them will have mercy.

PROVERBS 28:13

Beloved, if our heart does not condemn us, we have confidence toward God. And whatever we ask we receive from Him, because we keep His commandments and do those things that are pleasing in His sight.

1 JOHN 3:21–22

Blessed is he whose transgression is forgiven.

PSALM 32:1

There is no creature hidden from His sight, but all things are naked and open to the eyes of Him to whom we must give account.

HEBREWS 4:13

There is no soundness in my flesh
Because of Your anger,
Nor any health in my bones
Because of my sin.
For my iniquities have gone over my head;
Like a heavy burden they are too heavy for me.
My wounds are foul and festering
Because of my foolishness.

PSALM 38:3–5

CHAPTER 13

PRAYING TO FORGIVE YOURSELF, GOD, AND OTHERS

I struggled with forgiving my mother for years. Even after I became an adult she continued to be abusive, and I had to forgive her on a daily basis. Sometimes I stayed away from her and just let my dad deal with her by himself. Unfortunately she turned her anger toward him. When he became ill with a lung infection, instead of trying to help him, she would prepare her own meals and eat them in front of him without offering him anything. She said if he was hungry he could get up and get his own food.

When I found out all of this, I was very upset with her. What a turn of events. I had spent all those years trying to forgive her for being cruel to me, and now I had to forgive her for the way she treated my dad. There certainly didn't seem to be any way to change the situation. We'd tried to get my father to hospitalize my mother, but when he came to sign the papers, he couldn't do it. He still hoped that someday she would return to being the person he thought he had married.

Lord, I prayed, *I know my mother is mentally ill and doesn't really know what she is doing. But there is still something in me that thinks she does and that makes me mad. I again ask You to give me a forgiving heart toward her.*

The Lord answered that prayer time and again as each new offense brought more reasons to forgive. I know that I never could have heard God's leading for my life if my heart and mind had been clouded with unforgiveness.

STAIRWAY TO WHOLENESS

Forgiveness leads to life. Unforgiveness is a slow death. Not forgiving someone doesn't jeopardize your salvation and keep you out of heaven, but it does mean you won't enjoy all that God has for you. And you may find yourself wandering around outside the center of God's will.

The first step to forgiving is to *receive God's forgiveness* and let its reality penetrate the deepest part of your being. When we realize how much we have been forgiven, it's easier to understand that we have no right to pass judgment on one another. Being forgiven and released from everything we've ever done wrong is such a miraculous gift, how could we refuse to obey God when He asks us to forgive others as

He has forgiven us? Easy! We focus our thoughts on the person who has wronged us rather than on the God who makes all things right.

Forgiveness is a two-way street: God forgives you, and you forgive others. God forgives you quickly and completely upon your confession of wrongdoing. You are to forgive others quickly and completely, whether they admit failure or not. Most of the time people don't feel they've done anything wrong anyway, and if they do, they certainly don't want to admit it to you.

Forgiveness is a choice that we make. We base our decision not on what we *feel* like doing but on what we *know* is right. I did not *feel* like forgiving my mother. Instead I *chose* to forgive her because God's Word says, "Forgive, and you will be forgiven" (Luke 6:37). That verse also says that we shouldn't judge if we don't want to be judged ourselves.

I had to understand that God loves my mother as much as He loves me. He loves *all* people as much as He loves me. He loves the murderer, the rapist, the prostitute, and the thief. And He hates all of their sins as much as He hates ours. He hates murdering, raping, whoring, and stealing as much as He hates pride, gossiping, and unforgiveness. We may sit and compare our sins to other people's and say, "Mine aren't so bad," but God says they all stink, so we shouldn't worry about whose smell the worst. The most important thing to remember when it comes to forgiving is that *forgiveness doesn't make the other person right; it makes you free.*

FORGIVING YOURSELF AND GOD

While forgiving others is crucial, forgiveness is also need-ed in two other areas. One area is *forgiving yourself.* So many of us think, *I should be achieving this; I should be this kind of person; I should have done more than I have by this time in my life.* I certainly was burdened by these kinds of thoughts.

God is the only one who is perfect. We have to be able to say, "Self, I forgive you for not being perfect, and I thank You, God, that You are right now making me into all that You created me to be."

Some of us have to forgive ourselves for the mistakes we have made. Before I came to know the Lord, I wasted my life doing drugs, dabbling in the occult, and getting involved in unhealthy relationships. When I was finally able to forgive myself, I realized that God could use even those experiences for His glory. I am now able to speak into the lives of women who have committed these same errors. They see that what God has helped me to overcome is possible for them too.

Besides forgiving others and yourself, you must also check to see if you need to *forgive God.* If you've been mad at Him, say so. "God, I've been mad at You ever since my brother was killed in that accident." "God, I've been mad at You since my baby died." "God, I've been mad at You ever since I didn't get that job I prayed for." Be honest. You won't crush God's ego. Release the hurt and let yourself cry. Tears are freeing and healing. Say, "Lord, I confess my hurt and my anger, and my hardness of heart toward You. I no longer hold that against You."

Forgiveness is ongoing because once you've dealt with the past, constant infractions occur in the present. None of us get by without having our pride wounded or being manipulated, offended, or hurt by someone. Each time that happens it leaves a scar on the soul if not confessed and dealt with before the Lord. Besides that, unforgiveness also separates you from people you love. They sense a spirit of unforgiveness, even if they can't identify it, and it makes them uncomfortable and distant.

You may be thinking, *I don't have to worry about this because I have no unforgiveness toward anyone.* But forgiveness also has to do with not being critical of others. It has to do with keeping in mind that people are often the way they are because of how life has shaped them. I began to truly forgive my mother when I realized how difficult her childhood had been and what problems she had faced as she grew to adulthood. We all need to remember that God is the only one who knows the whole story, and therefore we never have the right to judge. Being chained in unforgiveness keeps you from the healing, joy, and restoration that are there for you. Being released into the future God has for you means letting go of all that has happened in the past.

PRAYERS

TO FORGIVE YOURSELF

Lord, I know that You have forgiven me for my sins of _____. I thank You for Your unconditional love and grace. I am truly repentant and wish to overcome these tendencies. Now, Father, help me forgive myself. Erase my guilt and create a new heart within me.

TO FORGIVE GOD

Lord, I admit that I am upset with You because of _____.

Help me see things from Your perspective. I know You are a good God and have my best interests in mind at all times. Forgive me for holding this against You. Heal me of my disappointment.

TO FORGIVE OTHERS

Lord, _____ has hurt me in this way: _____. I do not understand why this has happened, but I know that You want me to forgive (him/her). Help me walk in (his/her) shoes and understand what would make (him/her) do or say this. Help me be completely released from all unforgiveness.

TOOLS OF TRUTH

And whenever you stand praying, if you have anything against anyone, forgive him, that your Father in heaven may also forgive you your trespasses.

MARK 11:25

Let all bitterness, wrath, anger, clamor, and evil speaking be put away from you, with all malice. And be kind to one another, tenderhearted, forgiving one another, even as God in Christ forgave you.

EPHESIANS 4:31–32

Judge not, and you shall not be judged. Condemn not, and you shall not be condemned. Forgive, and you will be forgiven.

LUKE 6:37

He who loves his brother abides in the light, and there is no cause for stumbling in him. But he who hates his brother is in darkness and walks in darkness, and does not know where he is going, because the darkness has blinded his eyes.

1 JOHN 2:10–11

PART THREE

THE
OBEDIENT
WALK

CHAPTER 14

PRAYING TO SEE THE LINK BETWEEN OBEDIENCE AND BLESSING

I didn't want to move from California to Nashville. I had a great church, great friends, and a great home. But Michael felt differently. He had been commuting to Nashville a couple of times a month to work, and he had fallen in love with the city.

But I hadn't been to Nashville in twenty years, and I hadn't fallen in love with the town, so I was resistant. "If God is telling you to move to Nashville," I said to Michael, "why can't He tell me too?"

I was praying every week in my prayer group for God to show me His will, but I had not received an answer.

Two months later, I accompanied Michael on a business trip to Nashville. When I went to our room to rest before dinner, I couldn't sleep. I sensed the Lord saying, *You are supposed to be here.*

Is this really You, Lord? I prayed.

The more I lay there, the more I was sure the Lord was saying it was His will for us to make this move.

We did make the move a couple of months later, and we were glad we did because our house in California was destroyed by the Northridge earthquake. We were grateful that we had listened to God and obeyed Him when He gave us direction for our lives. It has been our greatest reminder that obedience and blessing go hand in hand.

BENEFITS OF OBEDIENCE

How many times do we ask God to give us what *we* want, but we don't want to give God what *He* wants? We lack what we desire most—wholeness, peace, fulfillment, and joy—because we are not obedient to God.

Often we are not obedient because we don't understand that God has set up certain rules to protect us and work for our benefit. The Ten Commandments were not given to instill guilt, but as an umbrella of blessing and protection from the rain of evil. If we choose to live outside the arena of blessing, spiritual darkness and confusion have access to our lives, and we are drained of God's best. When we obey, life has simplicity and clarity and unlimited blessing.

We *need* God's laws because we don't know how to make life work without them. The Bible says, "If anyone competes in athletics, he is not crowned unless he competes according to the rules" (2 Tim. 2:5). If restoration is the name of the game, then obedience is one of the rules. The more I've searched the Scriptures, the more I've found that the Bible is full of promises for those who obey God:

- *There is the promise of healing.* "Make straight paths for your feet, so that what is lame may not be dislocated, but rather be healed" (Heb. 12:13).

- *There is the promise of answered prayer.* "If I had cherished sin in my heart, the Lord would not have listened" (Ps. 66:18 NIV).

- *There is the promise of God fighting our battles for us.* "Oh, that My people would listen to Me, that Israel would walk in My ways! I would soon subdue their enemies, and turn My hand against their adversaries" (Ps. 81:13–14).

- *There is the promise of living a long life in peace.* "Let your heart keep my commands; for length of days and long life and peace they will add to you" (Prov. 3:1–2).

There are many more promises like these, and just as many warnings of what will *not* happen in our lives if we *don't* obey. After reading them, I felt inspired to ask God to show me exactly what I needed to be doing. He was quick to answer that prayer. *Check your heart,* He said. *Are you really willing to obey? If so, those promises are there for you—and all My children.*

THE CHOICE IS OURS—THE POWER IS HIS

I've learned that God doesn't enforce obedience. We often wish He would because it would be easier, but He gives us the choice. I had to ask Him to teach me to be obedient out of love for Him and desire to serve the One who has done so much for me. If you want the same benefits, you'll have to do the same thing. It helps to understand that the Lord is on your side and the call to obedience is *not* to make you feel like a hopeless failure if you don't do everything right.

The Bible says that Noah was given new life because he did *all* that God asked him to do (Gen. 6:22). The word *all* seems frightening when it comes to obedience because we know ourselves well enough to doubt we can do it all. And the truth is we can't. But we *can* ask God to enable us to take steps of obedience.

The minute we take one step of obedience, God opens up opportunities for new life. Unfortunately, the opposite is also true. The minute we start to think it's not necessary to obey, we have opened the door for evil. Oswald Chambers said, "If [a person] wants insight into what Jesus Christ teaches, he can only get it by obedience . . . spiritual darkness comes because of something I do not intend to obey."[1]

For anyone who has been emotionally wounded in any way, a certain amount of healing will happen in your life just by being obedient to God. The Bible says, "He who obeys instructions guards his life" (Prov. 19:16 NIV). The more obedient you are, the more bondage will be stripped away from your life. There is also a certain healthy confidence that comes from knowing you've obeyed God. This confidence builds self-worth and nourishes a broken personality.

When you are trying to know the will of God for your life, obedience to God's ways and God's directives are a must. You will never be in the center of God's will for your life if you are continually living in disobedience. There are many different areas of obedience, but I have included just eight basic steps that will get you headed in the right direction. They are a guideline, not a threat. Just take one step at a time, remembering that the power of the Holy Spirit in us enables us to obey God.

PRAYER

God, I don't want to be a person who collapses every time something shakes me. I don't want anything to separate me from Your presence and Your love. And I really do have a heart that wants to obey. Please show me where I am not living in obedience to You, and help me do what I need to do. I don't ever want to miss Your perfect will for my life because I have foolishly not obeyed You.

TOOLS OF TRUTH

Great peace have those who love Your law,
And nothing causes them to stumble.

PSALM 119:165

If you are willing and obedient,
You shall eat the good of the land.

ISAIAH 1:19

Do not merely listen to the word, and so deceive yourselves.
Do what it says.

JAMES 1:22 NIV

Therefore, to him who knows to do good and does not do
it, to him it is sin.

JAMES 4:17

He who says, "I know Him," and does not keep His commandments, is a liar, and the truth is not in him.

1 JOHN 2:4

CHAPTER 15

PRAYING TO SAY YES TO GOD EACH DAY OF YOUR LIFE

When you buy a house you first make a large down payment. Then, to keep the house, you must make a smaller payment every time it comes due. You can't change your mind and say, "I don't feel like making payments!" without serious consequences.

The same is true of your relationship with God. To make Him your permanent dwelling place, your initial down payment consists of making Him Lord over your life. After that, ongoing payments must be made, which means saying yes whenever God directs you to do something. They are all a part of the purchase, but one happens initially and the other is eternally ongoing (just like house payments!). The difference is that the Lord will take only as much payment from me as I am willing to give Him. And I can possess only as much of what He has for me as I am willing to secure with my obedience.

Taking the initial step of making Him Lord over your life is the same for everyone. Saying yes to God every day is an individual matter. God gives you personalized direction so He may ask you to do something He is not asking anyone else to do. For example, He may be directing you to leave a specific job or move to another city. You have to trust that God has your best interests in mind and be willing to do what He asks of you, even if you don't understand why at the time. Obedience starts with having a heart that says yes to God. We can never live in God's will if we haven't learned to say yes whenever God gives us direction for our lives.

RELEASING YOUR DREAMS

I always wanted to be a successful entertainer. It sounds embarrassingly shallow even to mention it now, but it was a desperate drive when I was younger. I desired to be famous and respected, never mind the fact that I possibly didn't have what it might take to attain either goal. After I received the Lord and had been married just a few months, God clearly impressed upon my heart that I wasn't to do television or commercials anymore. I wasn't sure why, but I knew it wasn't right for me. Whenever my agent presented me with an interview I would have previously died for, the thought of it gave me a hollow, uneasy, deathlike feeling. Because the peace of God did not accompany the prospect of doing it, I turned down every job that was offered.

Yes, God, I won't do that commercial. Yes, God, I won't accept another television show. Yes, God, I won't sing in clubs anymore. Yes, God, I'll leave the agency.

Gradually, all my work was gone. God had closed the doors and asked me to stop knocking on the ones that were not in His plan for me. The experience was scary, but looking back now I clearly see the reasons for it. Acting was an idol for me. I did it entirely for the attention and acceptance it would bring me, not because I loved the work. My identity was totally wrapped up in what I did. For God to change that, He had to take away my means of defining who I thought I was and help me establish my identity in Jesus. He knew I couldn't be healed of my deep inferiority feelings if I was daily putting myself in a position of being judged by superficial standards.

The part we don't want to hear is that a time comes when each of us must place our desires and dreams in the hands of God so that He might free us from those that are not His will. In other words, you secure your future by releasing your dream to God and, if need be, allowing it to die. If you've always had a certain picture of what you think you should do, you have to be willing to let the picture be destroyed. If it really is what God has for you, He will raise you up to do that and more. If it isn't, you will be frustrated as long as you cling to it.

Often the desires of *your* heart *are* the desires of *His* heart, but they still must be achieved *His* way, not yours, and you must know that it is He who is accomplishing them in you, not you achieving them yourself. *God wants us to stop holding on to our dreams and start holding on to Him so that He can enable us to soar above ourselves and our own limitations.* Whenever we let go of what we long for, God will bring it back to us in another dimension.

THE ART OF THE QUICK RESPONSE

Saying yes to God means being willing to obey *immediately* when we hear His voice, and not waiting until all else fails or we feel like it or we're at the end of ourselves. For God to transform us into whole people, we have to be totally available to Him. If He is telling us, "Do this," then our saying, "Yes, God" immediately will bring the desired results more quickly.

Again, this is done a step at a time. If you can't trust God enough yet to say, "Anything You ask of me, I'll do," then keep working at it. I must admit that saying yes to God was difficult for me until I read God's words in the Scripture: "When *I* called, *they* did not listen; so when *they* called, *I* would not listen" (Zech. 7:13 NIV, emphasis added). That puts it all in perspective, doesn't it? If we want God to hear our prayers, we need to listen and respond to His voice.

Being willing to say yes to God made me a candidate for much healing and blessing. Of course, I don't always hear Him and I don't always say yes immediately, but my desire is to do that. Saying yes to God without reservation is the first step of obedience that begins to build a successful and fulfilling life on the foundation you have laid down in the Word: prayer, confession, praise, and ongoing forgiveness.

PRAYER

Dear Lord, help me to continually say yes to You. Help me not be afraid to trust You and Your will for my life. I want to experience everything You have for me.

TOOLS OF TRUTH

Those who live according to the flesh set their minds on the things of the flesh, but those who live according to the Spirit, the things of the Spirit.

ROMANS 8:5

If anyone desires to come after Me, let him deny himself, and take up his cross daily, and follow Me. For whoever desires to save his life will lose it, but whoever loses his life for My sake will save it.

LUKE 9:23–24

Delight yourself also in the LORD,
And He shall give you the desires of your heart.

PSALM 37:4

You shall worship the LORD your God, and Him only you shall serve.

MATTHEW 4:10

I delight to do Your will, O my God.

PSALM 40:8

CHAPTER 16

PRAYING TO REMAIN SEPARATE FROM THE WORLD

The first time I heard Dolores Hayford speak, I knew Pastor Jack had inherited his gift of teaching from his mother. In a clear, gentle voice she told a story of her youngest son, Jim.

One day young Jim realized that some people have blessing upon blessing while others don't. He asked his mother, "Why do some people get all the breaks with God?"

After giving it some thought Mrs. Hayford said, "Son, those who get the breaks with God are the ones who first break from the world."

That piece of motherly advice stuck in my mind so strongly I pondered it for weeks afterward. *What exactly is the world?* I prayed to the Lord. *And how do I break away from it?*

Over the next few months of Bible study I came to see that the world is anything that sets itself against God and His ways.

The Bible says, "Whoever therefore wants to be a friend of the world makes himself an enemy of God" (James 4:4).

I knew I definitely didn't want to be God's enemy!

I also read, "Be sober, be vigilant; because your adversary the devil walks about like a roaring lion, seeking whom he may devour" (1 Peter 5:8). The Bible describes Satan as our "enemy," the "ruler of this world," and by aligning with the world's systems and ways of doing things, we are aligning with him.

In the past, I had rejected the idea of a personal devil as basically naive. Only the most foolish and ignorant people could support such nonsense. Besides, my occult practices had convinced me that evil existed only in people's minds. But the more I studied God's Word and saw its accuracy, the more I faced the reality of a dark and evil force controlling the lives of people who allow it. How could I deny that it existed when I could *see* it manifested in every form of evil in the world around me? Now I realize that the foolish and ignorant people are those who deny the satanic realm. *Breaking from the world means recognizing our enemy and refusing to be aligned with him in any way.*

THE RULES OF THIS WORLD

Time and time again in the Old Testament, a king who served the Lord in all other things would not destroy the high places where pagan gods were worshiped. As a result, he and his people did not enjoy all the blessing, protection, healing, and answered prayer that God had for them. They, like us, did not clearly identify their enemy and break completely from the world.

Our enemy is Satan, the ruler of this world, who was originally created beautiful, wise, and without sin. He had access to the throne of God, but fell from this high position when he chose to exert *his* will over God's. No one tempted him; he decided to rebel on his own. When his rebellion led to his expulsion from God's kingdom, he set himself to oppose all that God is and does.

But Satan is limited. He cannot be everywhere, he is not able to do everything, he is not all-powerful, and he is not all-knowing. God, on the other hand, is *all* of those things. What Satan and God *do* have in common is that they both have a plan for our lives, which can only be made operative if we submit to it. We don't have to fear Satan because the Bible says that "He who is in you is greater than he who is in the world" (1 John 4:4). Jesus' death on the cross has broken Satan's power, so we don't have to be intimidated by him.

There is no indication in the Bible that Satan can possibly win over God; God's power far surpasses his. The only success Satan can have comes through deception—getting us to believe he doesn't exist or that he is not our enemy, or instilling in us lies about ourselves, our situations, others, him, or God. Once we believe his lies, he controls our lives.

I worry when people tell me there is no such thing as a devil. I reflect on their lives—a marriage that is falling apart or a son on drugs or a teenage daughter having her second abortion or a husband's drinking problem or a mother's depression or a secret affair—and I think, *Dear person, there is nothing in your life to convince me that there is no devil.* Their situations are worse because they have an enemy and don't even know it. He will lead them down the path of destruction, and they will follow him and then blame God for what happens. The devil's plans for your life will succeed if you believe that he doesn't exist or that he is in any way on your side.

My friend Diane, who had been into occult practices with me, didn't want to get rid of her occult books or stop her occult practices when she accepted Jesus as her Savior. She thought she could mix a little bit of the occult with Christianity and have the best of both worlds. But the more she resisted giving up those practices, the more miserable and depressed she became. Nothing in her life seemed to be going right. She desperately wanted to have a child but couldn't get pregnant. She had difficulties in her marriage that caused her grief. She always felt that her prayers were not being answered.

I kept encouraging her to read the Bible for herself and attend church regularly. As she did, she began to see that she couldn't belong to both worlds—the devil's and God's. She had to choose one or the other. Finally she made the decision to throw away the books and separate herself from all occult associations and practices.

In the next few months after she made that decision, she and her husband began going to a Christian marriage counselor. Their relationship improved, and within a year she gave birth to her son, John. I don't think that was all a coincidence.

Those two things alone were miracles in her life and she recognized them as such. I don't believe they would have happened if she had not separated from the enemy's world and aligned herself with God's kingdom. Miracles don't happen when we have one foot inside the enemy's camp.

Accepting the world's standards for our lives numbs our sensitivity to God's will. It separates us from what He has called us to be. We reserve a place in our hearts to be the exception. We think, *I'm above the Lord's ways. I don't need to obey.* But that is what Satan said before he fell from heaven.

The way we combat this deception is simple. The Bible says, "Submit to God. Resist the devil and he will flee from you" (James 4:7). We need to separate ourselves from the world's habits and ways of thinking and destroy the high places of our hearts. We must tell Satan we refuse to believe his lies or do things his way. When we refuse Satan, the promise is, "The LORD will go before you, and the God of Israel will be your rear guard" (Isa. 52:12). The Lord will protect us from anything we may face ahead, and He will guard us against any dangers sneaking up from behind.

RUN A CHECK FOR HIGH PLACES

Breaking from the world doesn't require you to live like a hermit for the rest of your life. But you do have to run a frequent check on your heart to make sure that you are not too attached to the world. Ask yourself these questions:

- Do I judge myself by the world's standard for beauty, acceptability, and success?

- Do I depend on worldly magazines and books to tell me how to live?

- Am I willing to ignore certain convictions I have in order to find favor with other people?

- Am I drawn toward emulating in any way the lifestyles of celebrities rather than becoming who God created *me* to be?

- Am I willing to compromise what I know of God's ways in order to gain something I want?

If you said yes to any of those questions, you are cutting off the possibilities God has for your life. God asks, "Since you died with Christ to the basic principles of this world, why, as though you still belonged to it, do you submit to its rules?" (Col. 2:20 NIV). He clearly instructs us, "Do not be conformed to this world, but be transformed by the renewing of your mind, that you may prove what is that good and acceptable and perfect will of God" (Rom. 12:2).

Believe me, I know how hard it is to try to lay down everything in your life at once. Many of our high places have been erected for our own survival, and we may feel we still need them. But the more we allow God to reign in us, the easier it will be to let go of anything that exalts itself above Him.

I'm deliberately not making a list of "don'ts" because the point is for *you* to separate *yourself* in your heart. You will learn what particulars to eliminate as you seek God and pray in the way I suggest at the end of this chapter.

I never thought I opposed God, but I have learned that nearly everything I did before I received Jesus opposed His ways. We can make ourselves sick by being dissatisfied with what God gives us or by running after things that are not from Him. God wants to take all cravings for the world out of our hearts and replace them with a hunger for more of Jesus.

The Bible says, "Come out from among them and be separate" (2 Cor. 6:17). You can't go forward if you cling to things that separate you from God. It's a step of obedience that happens in the heart and paves the way for true spiritual well-being in the center of God's will.

PRAYER

Lord, if there are things in my life that are not of You, I don't want them. Please take them away and release me from longing for them. Help me draw on You for all my needs. Teach me to recognize my enemy and give me strength to resist him. Help me turn my heart away from the world and look only to You as my source and my guide.

TOOLS OF TRUTH

Do not love the world or the things in the world. If anyone loves the world, the love of the Father is not in him. For all that is in the world—the lust of the flesh, the lust of the eyes, and the pride of life—is not of the Father but is of the world. And the world is passing away, and the lust of it; but he who does the will of God abides forever.

1 JOHN 2:15–17

Let no one say when he is tempted, "I am tempted by God"; for God cannot be tempted by evil, nor does He Himself tempt anyone. But each one is tempted when he is drawn away by his own desires and enticed.

JAMES 1:13–14

That they may come to their senses and escape the snare of the devil, having been taken captive by him to do his will.

2 TIMOTHY 2:26

He who sins is of the devil, for the devil has sinned from the beginning. For this purpose the Son of God was manifested, that He might destroy the works of the devil.

1 JOHN 3:8

CHAPTER 17

PRAYING
TO BE
BAPTIZED

"We need to be baptized, Michael," I said late one evening shortly after Michael and I were married. We had been discussing Pastor Jack's sermon on baptism the day before and how Jesus Himself had been baptized by John the Baptist (Matt. 3:13–16).

For months I had seen people being baptized at the church on Sunday nights but had dismissed it as a religious ritual I didn't need. Besides, I had been baptized as a baby, as were all the children in our family. But at that Wednesday evening prayer meeting, Pastor Jack explained that baptism isn't just a ritual or optional meaningless tradition; it is a commandment of Jesus.

"Going against a tradition that is God-ordained brings trouble, and you jeopardize your fruitfulness by ignoring it," he said. "When you come to baptism, you are turning your back on your old life. You are saying, 'Lord, You have died for me, now I am dying to myself to receive Your life.' His death on the cross sealed the covenant from His side. Your response in baptism is saying, 'Lord, I seal the covenant from my side, but it's Your power that makes it work.'"

The more Michael and I talked about the fact that we were limiting what God could do in us and possibly bringing trouble into our lives by not being obedient, the more urgent it seemed. We prayed that God would help us take this step of obedience. "We should do it right away," he said to me after we had finished praying.

"How right away do you mean?" I responded.

"Tonight," he said firmly.

"Tonight? Where are we going to find someone who will baptize us tonight? It's after ten o'clock."

"Pat Boone baptizes people in his pool," he said enthusiastically.

"Pat Boone? In his pool? Does that count? Doesn't it have to be in a church? With a pastor?"

"It can be anywhere. And Pat Boone is a church elder. They baptize people at their house all the time."

"But does he do it at this hour?" I questioned further. We had attended some Bible studies at Pat and Shirley's house, but I wasn't sure they would welcome an unscheduled visit from us this late in the evening.

"Let's call him and find out," Michael said as he picked up the phone. Within ninety seconds the arrangements were made. We grabbed a change of clothes and were on our way.

The Boone house was a twenty-minute drive from ours, and on the way strong, cold October winds whipped our small car. I started to feel anxious and afraid.

"We must be doing something important," I said. "I keep hearing this voice in my head saying, 'This is stupid. Go home and go to bed. It's late. It's cold. This isn't necessary.'"

Still we kept on driving until we finally pulled into the circular driveway and parked near the front door. Once we were inside Pat's rambling two-story house, I felt safe. We had been in the enormous open den for prayer meetings or to hear visiting ministers speak, and I could always sense the presence of the Lord there.

The house was quiet, only a couple of rooms were lit, and Shirley and their four daughters were upstairs getting ready for bed. Pat didn't question the hour or give any indication that he was inconvenienced. The Holy Spirit who had prompted *our* hearts must have prepared *his* as well.

Michael and I sat on the couch and Pat sat on the floor in front of us. He talked for nearly a half an hour about the significance of what we were doing, reiterating much of Pastor Jack's message. Once Pat was convinced that we understood, he showed us to the small house outside where we changed into appropriate clothing. As we walked to the pool, the cold wind became violent, and I could barely control the large terry cloth towel I had wrapped around myself. The baptism took less than a minute, and when I came up out of the water the wind had quieted. I felt there was a definite correlation in the spirit realm.

We had waited a long time to take this step of obedience because we hadn't understood its importance. I'm still not sure I understand it all today, but I *do* understand that right after that, our spiritual growth proceeded more quickly. And I felt a new joy in my heart from knowing I had obeyed the Lord.

A BABY STEP OF GIANT SIGNIFICANCE

Baptism is a very simple first step in learning to obey God, and it only has to be done once if you understand what you're doing. But if the baptism had no meaning for you (either because you were a baby or had no relationship with the Lord), you need to be baptized now. While you are not negating anything you did as a child or when you didn't know the Lord, you are now saying, "I let my life, as I have always lived it, be buried in the water. I enter a stream where the power of the Holy Spirit carries me. I place God as captain over my life and desire that He navigate me where I should go. I now live in the power of His life."

Jesus Himself was baptized in order to do what was right and He commanded us all to do the same, saying, "He who believes and is baptized will be saved" (Mark 16:16). It can't be any clearer. Baptism in water is an act of obedience to declare the lordship of Jesus in your life.

While there is no magic in the water, you are not simply

getting wet either. Whether you feel it at the time or not, the strongholds of your past have been broken in the spirit realm. You may not observe anything different about the weather as I did and you may not see a single dove or hear God's voice as Jesus did, but you can trust that the Holy Spirit of God has descended upon you and will open up the kingdom of God to you.

I've known some believers who suffer with horribly painful wounds from their past, but they refuse to take this simple step. I'm not even sure why. One girl came to me for advice, and I went through these foundational steps with her, but she refused to do this one. Year after year I see her still suffering, still having problems in her marriage, still dealing with anger and unforgiveness, still battling depression. All because she has not made a total commitment to living God's way.

Don't let Satan rob you of what God has for you by convincing you, "It's not important." "You'll look silly." "This is a meaningless ritual." "There's no power in this." Reject those lies. Even if you've been a Christian for thirty years and a leader in your church, don't let pride keep you from receiving what God has for you. If you're an invalid or handicapped or in a hospital or nursing home, have someone call a pastor to come to you to baptize you. If you're in prison, tell the chaplain you want to be baptized or find a believer who has been baptized and have him pour water on your head and baptize you in the name of the Father, the Son, and the Holy Spirit. The power is not in the water; it's in your desire to obey God's Word and the Lord Jesus' command. God doesn't take a magic wand and wave it over your life like a fairy god-mother. He wants more for you than that. He wants to walk *with* you hand in hand and give you keys of authority to live victoriously in this life.

PRAYER

Dear Lord, I want to obey You in every way. Help me take all the necessary steps to do it. Break any pride, skepticism, doubt, or fear that keeps me from taking steps of obedience as Your Word commands.

TOOLS OF TRUTH

Then Peter said to them, "Repent, and let every one of you be baptized in the name of Jesus Christ for the remission of sins; and you shall receive the gift of the Holy Spirit."

ACTS 2:38

Or do you not know that as many of us as were baptized into Christ Jesus were baptized into His death? Therefore we were buried with Him through baptism into death, that just as Christ was raised from the dead by the glory of the Father, even so we also should walk in newness of life.

ROMANS 6:3–4

When He had been baptized, Jesus came up immediately from the water; and behold, the heavens were opened to Him, and He saw the Spirit of God descending like a dove and alighting upon Him.

MATTHEW 3:16

And now why are you waiting? Arise and be baptized, and wash away your sins, calling on the name of the Lord.

ACTS 22:16

CHAPTER 18

PRAYING TO HAVE
FELLOWSHIP WITH
OTHER BELIEVERS

One evening, years after we were married, Michael and I had a heated argument as we were getting ready to go to a friend's house for dinner. We had misinterpreted each other's intentions and said words that were hurtful and pain-provoking. I was reduced to tears and he to silence.

Great! I thought. *The last thing I want to do feeling like this is be with other people.* I silently ran through a list of reasons we could possibly cancel, but they sounded too feeble so I resigned myself to the evening.

During the entire drive to our host's home we sat in silence, except for Michael's asking, "Are you not going to speak to me all night?" To which I cleverly replied, "Are you not going to speak to *me* all night?"

I started thinking about the couple we were going to visit.

Bob and Sally Anderson were one of the first Christian couples Michael and I had befriended after we were married. We had a lot in common, including our children. Their daughter, Kristen, and our son, Christopher, were born about the same time and had become good friends. We loved being with them because they were solid in their relationship as well as their faith, and we knew there weren't going to be any weird surprises in store for us.

From the moment we arrived at their home I felt the tension between Michael and me dissipate. Throughout the evening our hearts softened, and by the time we went home we were laughing. It was as if the goodness of the Lord in the Anderson family had rubbed off on us and we were strengthened by it.

This kind of thing happened so many times that when Pastor Jack exhorted us to "be in fellowship with other believers" and waved his hand across the congregation as if to get his sheep moving, I understood the need for it.

MORE THAN JUST FRIENDSHIP

The word *fellowship* sounded strange and "churchy" when I first heard it. It reminded me of tea and cookies after a missionary meeting or a potluck dinner in the church basement. I've since discovered it's much more than just coffee hour. The dictionary definition is "companionship, a friendly association, mutual sharing, a group of people with the same interests." In the biblical sense, it's even more than that.

"Fellowship has to do with a mutuality in all parts of your life," Pastor Jack taught us. "You bear one another's burdens and fulfill the law of Christ. You pray for one another, you love one another, you help one another when there is material need, you weep with those who weep and rejoice with those who rejoice. It's growing in an association with people who are moving in the same pathway you are and sharing with each other in your times of victory or need or your times of trial or triumph. It's growing in relationship."

Fellowship is instrumental in shaping us. The Bible says that we become like those we spend time with and good friends sharpen one another just as iron sharpens iron (Prov. 27:17). This is reason enough to spend time with other believers, but there is even more to it.

INSIDE THE CHURCH

First and most basic of all, it is very important that you find a church home and spend time with that body of believers in church. I certainly understand if you have been hurt or burned out by a church, but please hear me out. No two churches are alike. Each has its own personality. Some are great, some good, and some not quite what you hoped they'd be. Somewhere there is a church that is right for you, and you need to ask God to help you find it.

Contrary to what some people think, the church doesn't have to have a fancy building. You can find a good church wherever a body of believers meet with a pastoral leader who is *also* submitted to *other* pastoral leadership. They must believe the Bible is the Word of God and offer good, solid teaching from it.

The next important indication of a good church is that you sense the love of God there and you receive it in abundance from the people. Some churches make an outgoing display of love, yet others who are more reserved may be just as genuine. If you pick up feelings of pride, competition, selfishness, self-righteousness, or coldness, determine whether that is the overall atmosphere or an isolated case. Remember that in any church you could find someone to exemplify these traits. Ask yourself if you *generally* feel love and acceptance there. You also need to be aware that you can't go into a church and *demand* that people love and care for you. You can communicate your needs, but you can't dictate how others should relate to you.

If you go to a church that doesn't believe in being born again or being baptized, you need to find a church that does. If the pastor can't bring himself to talk about the Holy Spirit working in power in your life and the members of the congregation don't praise and worship the Lord, you haven't found the right place yet. God can't work as powerfully in a church that limits Him and doesn't practice certain basic steps of obedience. Continue to look until you've found a solid church you can call home.

If you are in a church where you're miserable, get out. It's hard to receive God's love and life from a church you detest. This is not license to "church hop" whenever the pressure to grow is on, but don't fall for the "Now we gotcha!" trap either. Leave any church that tries to control your every breath.

Ask God to lead you to the right place. When you find it, make a commitment to stay and watch yourself grow. Go as often as you can. If once a week feels like a major commitment, start there. If once a week is easy, then go to midweek services also. Once you accept Jesus, you have eternal life whether you ever go to church or not, but I'm talking about living in the fullness of all God has for you. I'm talking about expelling the pain from deep within and living in love, peace, and joy. I'm talking about doing God's will. Certain visitations of God's power happen only in the midst of such gatherings of believers. Make it a point to be a part of that.

OUTSIDE THE CHURCH

There is also strength in being with believers *outside* the church. When you make friends with people who follow the Lord, there is a strong bond of love that makes other relationships seem shallow. Such friendships are the most fulfilling and healing. They can also be the most frustrating because we expect *Christians* to be perfect when in reality only *Christ* is perfect.

It's helpful to think of all fellowship with believers as beneficial: the pleasant encounters are *healing* and the unpleasant ones are *stretching*. When you run across believers who stretch you more than you feel you can handle, don't turn away from God. Remember, He is still perfect and good even if some of His children aren't. God always loves and respects you, even if a few of His offspring don't. I know that nothing hurts worse than a wound inflicted by a brother or sister in the Lord. Having been wounded many times like that myself, I am forced to remember that we will be imperfect until we go to be with Jesus. So we need to be merciful to those who "stretch" us and forgive quickly. Besides, we are probably stretching others ourselves.

The Bible says we should "not be unequally yoked together with unbelievers" (2 Cor. 6:14), but this doesn't mean you have to avoid them. It just means that your closest relationships, the ones that deeply touch and change your life, need to be with believers. Ask yourself, *Am I a godly influence in the lives of my unbelieving friends?* If so, then consider the relationship good. However, if they influence you away from God and His ways, then cut off the relationships immediately.

If your spouse is not a Christian, don't let his or her negative response to Jesus keep you from receiving the Lord's restoration for you. Check around for a Christian prayer group, Bible study, or a group with similar interests. I know someone who joined a Christian arts and crafts group and found great healing.

Start somewhere. Make a phone call to another believer and ask for prayer. Meet someone for lunch and talk about what the Lord has done in your life. Open up and extend yourself in some way. You may feel you don't have anything to share, but if you have the Lord, He's all you need.

If our first goal in any relationship is our own fulfillment, we will ultimately be let down or disappointed. As painful as it is, we have to give up that desire and lay it at Jesus' feet. However, there may be times when we have done all we can do in a relationship and it is still filled with problems. As hard as we try to make things good, a certain person may always leave you feeling depressed, angry, insecure, frightened, or hurt. When that happens, it is best to let the friendship go and give it to God to restore or remove as He sees fit.

Fellowship is a step of obedience that expands our hearts, bridges gaps, and breaks down walls. It encourages, fulfills, and balances our lives. All of this is necessary for spiritual well-being and a fruitful life in the will of God.

PRAYER

Lord, I acknowledge my need for other people. I ask You to lead me to relationships whereby I might grow in You and Your will might be fulfilled in me. Show me what steps to take to see that come about.

TOOLS OF TRUTH

Let us consider one another in order to stir up love and good works, not forsaking the assembling of ourselves together, as is the manner of some, but exhorting one another.

HEBREWS 10:24–25

Practice hospitality.

ROMANS 12:13 NIV

Do not be unequally yoked together with unbelievers.

2 CORINTHIANS 6:14

But if we walk in the light as He is in the light, we have fellowship with one another, and the blood of Jesus Christ His Son cleanses us from all sin.

1 JOHN 1:7

CHAPTER 19

PRAYING TO KNOW
HOW TO GIVE
YOURSELF AWAY

When I was ten years old, I lay awake in the middle of a cold, pitch-black night because I was too hungry to sleep. The pangs in my stomach were magnified by the knowledge that there was no food in the house and no money to buy any. My mother was asleep in the only other bedroom, on the opposite side of the house beyond the porch, and I felt isolated, alone, and afraid.

"There's nothing to eat," I had said to her earlier that evening after I searched the tiny kitchen. All I saw in the refrigerator were half-empty bottles of ketchup and mayonnaise. She had thrown remnants of old leftovers on the table for dinner—none of which went together in any appealing way—and made no apology for the fact that it wasn't enough to sustain either one of us.

"Stop your complaining. We don't have money for food," she snapped and went back to talking to herself the way she often did for hours at a time. She hated it when I intruded on her imaginary world.

Now, as I lay in bed, my mind reeled with fear about the future. I feared I could starve to death and no one would care. I felt old.

Going hungry was terribly frightening. Having to be totally dependent for life and sustenance upon someone I couldn't depend on at all bred deep insecurity. I'm sure now that my mother knew Dad would bring money when he came home, but she told me there was nothing at all to eat and no way to buy it and that was that. We had no friends, and Mother always made it seem as if we had no family either, since she considered them all to be her enemies. I had *nowhere* to turn and *no one* to help me. We had nothing to sell, and as far as I could see we had no prospects for making any money. I became desperately afraid for my future.

Once I was out of school and self-supporting, I handled money very carefully. I felt the weight of being entirely responsible for my life, and the horror of someday starving to death always bubbled just below the surface of my mind. After I came to know the Lord and started going to church, I put money in the collection plate according to what I had with me—a couple of dollars at first, then a five, a ten, and later a twenty. It was more like I was donating to a good cause or tipping the piano player than having any thought of actually giving to God. But when I heard Pastor Jack teach on what the Bible says about giving, I knew I had far more to learn about the subject than I ever dreamed.

I learned first of all that giving was actually giving *back* to God from out of what He had given me, and by doing so I would never lose anything. In fact, I would be enriched. I also learned that the Bible teaches we are to give a tithe (10 percent) of our income to the Lord. When I started doing that, I found that my financial blessings were greater and the drains on my finances were fewer. I found, too, that the more I gave, the less fear I had about not having enough. My future felt more secure. Because I experienced such a flow of God's blessing in my life, the thought of *not* giving became more frightening than giving.

Giving is a step of obedience that brings life, health, healing, and abundance. Not giving will stop up our lives and our bodies and eventually lead to emotional and physical sickness and poverty. The Bible says that a person who gives will have a secure heart and will triumph over his foes. There are two types of giving that are important: giving *to the Lord* and giving *as unto the Lord*.

GIVING TO THE LORD

Because we can't separate our money from our lives, God must be made Lord over our finances, and we must obey Him. God says in His Word that we need to give a tenth of our earnings back to Him for His purposes. When we realize that every cent we have comes from God in the first place, that's not such an unreasonable request. A good steward of money realizes he has nothing on his own, but only manages what he has been given.

If we tithe, the Bible promises we will receive a multiplied return of God's abundance and His power. The Lord asks us to try Him and see if He is not faithful to provide more blessings than we can contain. When we cut ourselves off from this life principle, the devourer comes in to eat up everything we have. I see people who don't give and then lose what they could have given in medical bills, appliance and car repairs, and a general lack of power to change their lives. God still loves them, but they've stopped up the flow of His blessing to them. The only way the storehouse of God's abundance can be opened is for them to start the process by opening themselves up to giving.

We often feel we will lose something if we give. We think, *If I didn't have to give this, I would have more for myself.* But actually that attitude will cause us to lose. The Bible says that if we give to the Lord, we will have everything we need in our lives. If we don't, we won't.

When Michael and I decided to move to Tennessee, we were advised to delay our relocation until we sold our California home. But we felt absolutely certain we were to go immediately, and so we moved and bought a house in Tennessee. Soon we had double mortgages, double taxes, double heating and cooling bills. We thought we were going to be buried under the financial strain. During those months we prayed that God would send the right buyer to us. We couldn't understand why the California house didn't sell until after the earthquake happened; then we realized that God had spared not only our lives, but He had spared the lives of anyone who would have been living in the house at that time.

Although we had earthquake insurance, it didn't cover everything and so we still lost a lot of money. But we didn't count the loss. We rejoiced that no one was injured or killed in that house. Through that whole time we continued to tithe and give as God directed us. And God took care of us over the following years and eventually restored all that we had lost.

GIVING AS UNTO THE LORD

Besides giving *to* the Lord, we need to get into the habit of giving to others *as unto* the Lord. This means we are to bless others because it blesses God — without expecting something in return. What-will-I-get-back thinking sets us up for disappointment and unhappiness, but when we give and expect nothing in return, the Lord rewards us.

Giving is a principle of release: "Give, and it will be given to you: good measure, pressed down, shaken together, and running over will be put into your bosom. For with the same measure that you use, it will be measured back to you" (Luke 6:38). To receive things that last, you must give from what you have. If you need release in any area, give something away of yourself, your possessions, or your life, and you will see things begin to open up to you.

There is much to give besides money or store-bought gifts. We can give food, clothing, services, time, prayer, assistance, a ride in our car, or any possession or ability that could help someone else. It's important, however, to ask God for wisdom and direction about giving. Once my husband and I gave money to a person in need and, instead of feeding his family and paying his rent, he spent it on drugs. We've learned to use careful discernment and seek God's guidance in giving to serve His purposes.

You may be so depleted that you feel you have nothing to give, or so overwhelmed by circumstances that giving of your-self seems monumental. If so, pray, "I don't feel that I have anything to give, Lord. Provide me with resources beyond myself." As long as you have the Lord in your life, you will always have at least one thing to give—His love. People need someone to love them, to listen, to encourage, and to pray for them. You might say to someone, "My gift to you is a promise to pray for you every day for a month." Who wouldn't love that gift? I know I would.

When we live in fear that we won't have enough, it's hard to give. But the truth is, the more we give to others, the more will be released to us. We will reap a spiritual as well as a material harvest. While it's good to save and plan wisely for the future because extreme poverty is emotionally crippling, giving to the Lord and to others must not be excluded. If we don't give as the Lord directs, we end up losing what we think we're saving anyway.

My mother never gave anything away, and I believe that was part of her mental and emotional illness. She hoarded everything out of fear that she would someday need it. Her closets, sheds, rooms, and garages were full of "stuff." The

Bible says, "He who gathered much had nothing left over, and he who gathered little had no lack" (2 Cor. 8:15). The sheer volume of my mother's stuff rendered it unusable.

Whenever my life seems to be stalled, deliberately giving of myself always brings breakthrough. It's not a matter of giving to get, but of taking this step of obedience to release the flow of all God has for you. It's not that you can't receive any of God's blessings unless you give but that you can't receive *all* of them and life becomes more of a struggle. And you can't be in the will of God if you don't give, because giving *is* the will of God. And giving releases blessings into your life that may seem entirely unrelated.

PRAYERS

FOR GIVING TO GOD
Lord, help me give the way You want me to, because I want to be obedient in this area of my life. Help me always tithe so that I am never robbing You of what is Yours. I want to live in the center of Your will so I can receive all You have for me and become all You made me to be.

FOR GIVING TO OTHERS
Dear Lord, show me any area of need where I could give something of myself or what I have. Show me what I might release of my life into the life of another person, and help me do it.

TOOLS OF TRUTH

You shall surely give to him, and your heart should not be grieved when you give to him, because for this thing the LORD your God will bless you in all your works and in all to which you put your hand.

DEUTERONOMY 15:10

But this I say: He who sows sparingly will also reap sparingly, and he who sows bountifully will also reap bountifully. So let each one give as he purposes in his heart, not grudgingly or of necessity; for God loves a cheerful giver.

2 CORINTHIANS 9:6–7

Blessed is he who considers the poor;
The LORD will deliver him in time of trouble.
The LORD will preserve him and keep him alive,
And he will be blessed on the earth;
You will not deliver him to the will of his enemies.
The LORD will strengthen him on his bed of illness;
You will sustain him on his sickbed.

PSALM 41:1–3

There is one who scatters, yet increases more;
And there is one who withholds more than is right,
But it leads to poverty.
The generous soul will be made rich,
And he who waters will also be watered himself.

PROVERBS 11:24–25

CHAPTER 20

PRAYING TO
BE REMINDED OF
JESUS' SACRIFICE

When I was thirteen, we left our run-down house behind the gas station where my father worked and found a home in a better neighborhood. Whenever we moved, my mother's mental condition improved somewhat, and for a short time she acted as if she had a new lease on life. Looking back, I believe she tried hard to pull herself together at those times, but her mental confusion was far too overpowering for her to withstand it alone. Before long she lost the battle and retreated to her make-believe world again.

During this one brief reprieve, when our lives temporarily resembled normalcy, Mother took my baby sister Suzy and me to a nearby church. Although the godhood of Christ was taught there, I don't remember any emphasis on a personal relationship with Jesus. I do remember that the Communion service was formal and beautiful and moved me to tears each time I heard about Jesus' suffering. I thought, *How cruel to have tortured and killed this good man,* as I closely related to His unjustified punishment.

That church experience didn't last very long because my mother soon fell back into her old reclusive ways. It was the last time any of us went to church until I came to the Church on the Way years later. There, two distinctly different aspects of the Communion service impressed me. First, it was called the *Lord's* Table. It was considered *His* table, not ours. It was *He* who invited us, not the church. Second, Communion was a joyful celebration of what Jesus accomplished for us on the cross as opposed to a mournful commemoration of His suffering. Pastor Jack called it "a celebration of victory, a reminder of Jesus' complete victory over our adversary, the enemy."

Pastor Jack's words resounded in my soul when he explained, "What Jesus says about the Lord's Table is 'I was broken for you, I bled and died for you, and I want you to never forget the deliverance and the victory and the triumph that it's intended to give you all the time. Because I did that, you don't have to be bound up in suffering and agony and hellishness. I want you to partake of that regularly and make it, every time, an annunciation of My triumph so that you're reminded of it.'"

Each time I took Communion, it reminded me that whatever I needed in my life had already been provided on the cross. The battle I faced had already been won!

A JOYFUL REMINDER

Communion is a step of obedience to Jesus, who said, "Do this in remembrance of Me" (Luke 22:19). If there were no other reason, that would be enough. But it also serves to remind us that Jesus forgives, heals, and delivers and that no power of sin, sickness, or Satan can prevail among those who lift up the power of Jesus' death in Communion. We partake of the Lord's Table to acknowledge joyfully what He accomplished for us personally on the cross so it will become a part of us. God knows we have short memories and need to be reminded frequently.

Just as there is no magic in the water of baptism, there is also nothing magical in the wine, grape juice, bread, or cracker of Communion. The power lies in our participation. That's why it's good to take Communion regularly—at least once a month if possible, or as often as the Lord prompts you. If you can't get to a Communion service in your church, then do it at home by yourself. All you need is a small amount of grape juice and a piece of bread or a cracker. (While it's true that Jesus and His disciples drank wine at the time of the Last Supper, many churches substitute grape juice for wine.)

As you eat the bread or cracker, remember that it is symbolic of His body, which was broken so your life could be mended. You are taking into yourself His wholeness so you can be nourished to become the whole person He made you to be. As you drink the wine or juice, remember that His blood was shed so you could be forgiven and not have to live in the consequences of sin.

Fortunately, the blessings of receiving Communion don't depend on our full comprehension of what it means. God says we will never understand His ways completely. As long as we take Communion without allowing it to dissolve into a religious ritual and as long as we ascribe the proper worth to what Jesus did on the cross, there is power in simply being obedient in this step, too.

PRAYER

Dear Jesus, I thank You for Your sacrifice for me. I know that You gave Your life that I might live eternally. Help me always comprehend the full worth of what You did on the cross every time I take Communion. And may I live fully in the victory You have secured.

TOOLS OF TRUTH

The Lord Jesus on the same night in which He was betrayed took bread; and when He had given thanks, He broke it and said, "Take, eat; this is My body which is broken for you; do this in remembrance of Me."

In the same manner He also took the cup after supper, saying, "This cup is the new covenant in My blood. This do, as often as you drink it, in remembrance of Me." For as often as you eat this bread and drink this cup, you proclaim the Lord's death till He comes.

Therefore whoever eats this bread or drinks this cup of the Lord in an unworthy manner will be guilty of the body and blood of the Lord. But let a man examine himself, and so let him eat of the bread and drink of the cup. For he who eats and drinks in an unworthy manner eats and drinks judgment to himself, not discerning the Lord's body. For this reason many are weak and sick among you, and many sleep.

1 CORINTHIANS 11:23–30

CHAPTER 21

PRAYING TO
BE ABLE TO
WALK IN FAITH

What if this Jesus thing is all a hoax? I thought to myself in horror one day nearly two years after I accepted Christ as Savior. *What if none of it's true? What if the pastor suddenly says, "This is all a joke, and you fell for it! Jesus isn't real and you're not really saved!"*

That day a wall of doubt settled around me like steel bars separating me from my future. The possibility of a life of nothingness became a temporary reality, and I panicked. *What brought this on all of a sudden?* I wondered. I struggled with that flash of doubt for days, and the more I thought about it, the more unhappy I became. I knew I had to reevaluate everything.

What was your life like before you met Jesus? I asked myself.

I was dying inside, I replied.

How did you feel? I questioned further.

Full of pain, hopelessness, and fear, I answered.

Are things better now?

Much.

What's different?

I don't feel depressed, fearful, or hopeless, I answered.

When did that change?

When I received Jesus, I started to feel better.

Your experience with the Lord was real? I asked.

Well, yes, I think so.

Then what's your problem? I asked.

The problem is I can't prove that Jesus is real.

Can you prove that He isn't?

No, I answered.

Well, then it looks like the choice is up to you, doesn't it? To believe or not to believe. It's your decision.

It's my decision, I answered.

Yes!

Okay, then. Weighing the quality of my life before I met Jesus against the quality of my life since then, I choose to believe Him.

Are you sure? I asked.

Yes. I have decided to follow Jesus. No turning back. No turning back.

This little scenario happened five or six times in the first ten years of my walk with the Lord. In retrospect, I believe it occurred in busy and stressful times when I had not spent enough time in the Word of God or had neglected being alone with the Lord in prayer and praise. Eventually I realized that sending a doubting spirit to torment us is one of the devil's favorite tactics.

WITHOUT A DOUBT

Faith is a spiritual muscle that needs to be exercised in order to prevent atrophy, which makes our entire spiritual being weak. Faith is first a decision, then an exercise in obedience, then a gift from God as it is multiplied. Our first step of faith is taken when we decide we will receive Jesus. After that, every time we decide to trust the Lord for anything, we build that faith. And whenever we decide *not* to trust Him, we tear it down. Faith is our daily decision to trust God.

The Bible says, "Whatever is not from faith is sin" (Rom. 14:23). How much clearer can it be? Faith is obedience. Doubt is disobedience. Faith is a gift from God because He enables us to believe, but we have to obey by building on that faith.

Scripture also says that a person who doubts is unstable in every way and cannot please God. If that's true, spiritual well-being is not possible without faith. To bolster your own faith, read through the fifteen characteristics of faith on the next page.

FIFTEEN CHARACTERISTICS OF FAITH

1. Faith is a choice.
2. Faith is a step of obedience.
3. Faith is a spiritual exercise.
4. Faith is taking God at His word.
5. Faith is saying yes to God.
6. Faith is looking to Jesus for everything.
7. Faith is knowing we are never without hope.
8. Faith is what lifts us out of our circumstances.
9. Faith is not holding anything back from God.
10. Faith is being obedient even if we don't feel like it.
11. Faith is a gift from God as we read His Word.
12. Faith is knowing that everything will work out.
13. Faith is a way out of our limitations.
14. Faith is the mother of hope.
15. Faith is the road to peace.

BUILT ON THE WORD

How do we start building faith? Once we have a little, how do we get more? The first step is to be totally open and honest about any doubt in God's ability or His faithfulness to provide for our every need. Oswald Chambers said, "Faith is unutterable trust in God, trust which never dreams He would not stand by us."[1] Doubt emanates from a lie of the enemy, which says God is not all-powerful. If you've listened to this lie, confess it as sin.

The next step is to fill your mind with the Word: "Faith comes from hearing the message, and the message is heard through the word of Christ" (Rom. 10:17 NIV). Reading the Word daily, regularly submitting to Bible teaching, and speaking the Word aloud will build faith. Your mouth and heart have to be united in this. One can't be saying, "God can," while the other says, "God can't." Your mind will convince your heart as you read or speak God's Word.

Whenever I'm afraid or doubt that my life is secure, I read the Bible until I sense God's peace in me. The more I read, the more hope I have. Then, when I pray, I'm confident that God will answer my prayers.

Even if you are not given to fear and doubt, you can be attacked by a *spirit of doubt,* as I was. When that happens, don't carry it by yourself. Take it to the Lord immediately. Or ask a mature believer to pray with you if you need to.

Sensing your own limitations doesn't mean you don't have faith. Feeling that *God* has limitations is what indicates a lack of faith. When faith has blossomed, it gives birth to hope, and says, "There is an end to this. I won't be in this situation forever. I won't always feel like this. I won't always hurt." Hope and faith together give you a vision for your life.

The Bible says of the people who could not go into the

Promised Land, "They could not enter in because of unbelief" (Heb. 3:19). Don't let that happen to you. Choose to enter in to all that God has for you by taking this important step of obedience.

PRAYER

Lord, I have made a decision to follow You. I know You hear my prayers even if I don't see the answers right away. No matter what happens, I am certain that I am not without hope. I have faith, but, Lord, strengthen my faith where it is weak.

TOOLS OF TRUTH

Without faith it is impossible to please Him, for he who comes to God must believe that He is, and that He is a rewarder of those who diligently seek Him.

HEBREWS 11:6

Let him ask in faith, with no doubting, for he who doubts is like a wave of the sea driven and tossed by the wind. For let not that man suppose that he will receive anything from the Lord; he is a double-minded man, unstable in all his ways.

JAMES 1:6–8

But the message they heard was of no value to them, because those who heard did not combine it with faith.

HEBREWS 4:2 NIV

Trust in the LORD with all your heart,
And lean not on your own understanding.

PROVERBS 3:5

Count it all joy when you fall into various trials, knowing that the testing of your faith produces patience.

JAMES 1:2–3

CHAPTER 22

PRAYING TO FIND
COMFORT IN THE CENTER
OF GOD'S WILL

As I have made this prayerful walk to spiritual well-being throughout the years, I have received many blessings from the Lord. One special blessing was my friendship with Diane, my friend whom I led to the Lord as we talked on the phone.

Diane and I had met in drama class in high school and immediately became good friends. We found we shared similar experiences with our mothers. As a result, we each grew up with deep fears, insecurities, feelings of being abandoned, and a severe lack of maternal nurturing. Neither of us ever brought friends home from school because we never knew what condition we would find our mothers in once we got there.

We went on to attend different colleges, but afterward we shared an apartment in Hollywood where we both pursued acting careers. We also shared the same spiritual walk. When one of us was into some occult practice or Eastern religion, the other got into it with the same enthusiasm. After we both had received the Lord, we spent even more time together. We shared ups and downs through our marriages and the births of our children. My two children were four years apart and her son, John, was right in between them in age. So they were a happy little trio whenever they were together. In fact, our families spent every holiday together.

When John was six, Diane was diagnosed with breast cancer. Our two families were devastated. She went through one miserable operation and treatment after another, and all the while we continued to pray for her healing. But then one terrible day, our worst fears were confirmed. The cancer had spread to her glands, stomach, bones, and brain.

"I just wanted to see John grow up," Diane sobbed to me when she called to report the doctor's diagnosis.

That summer, as Diane's illness progressed, I took care of John so Diane's husband could take care of her and still fulfill his business obligations. Also, Diane was suffering terribly and she didn't want John to remember her as she was in those last days. I kept praying for God's will to be done in Diane's life. We all wanted her healed. But we couldn't stand to see the agony she had to endure hour by hour every day.

A few days before Diane died I went to see her in the hospital. She could hardly talk because she was extremely nauseated and in a great deal of pain. Her beautiful eyes were almost expressionless. I put a cool cloth on her forehead, gave her some pieces of ice for the dryness in her throat, and applied a lip balm to her parched lips.

Then I asked her if she had written a letter to John. We had talked about this in the last few months, but Diane had been hesitant to do it. I knew why. The letter was so final. It meant that she knew she was dying, and she wanted to do everything she could to avoid facing that possibility. But this time she nodded that she had indeed written the letter and she told me where to find it.

The week John was born, Diane and her husband had asked me if I would agree to take care of him if anything ever happened to them. I of course said yes, and John was left to us in their will. That day in the hospital she asked me again. I assured her I would always take care of him.

John was eight when Diane died. For months after her death I kept him with us during the week. Early Monday morning his dad would bring John to us and then return for him on Friday night. I always hated to see him go.

The following year, John and his dad moved to Oregon where his dad could work out of his home and be with John full-time. We missed them, but we were still able to see them every holiday and summer vacation for the next few years.

Then one afternoon, I received a phone call from the Oregon police. John's dad had been killed in an automobile accident, and at the age of sixteen John was an orphan. How our hearts broke for him again.

That fall John became our spiritually adopted son, and I became his legal guardian. He had always been like a brother to my children and he had been like my own son. Now the relationship was official.

How blessed we were to have him as part of our family. He was the missing piece we didn't even know was missing. God knew we needed someone to complete our family. We all loved him, but I especially cherished him because he reminded me so much of his mom. He had her intelligence and wit, as well as some of her mannerisms and expressions.

Through all of this, I have learned that having painful and difficult things happen to you doesn't mean you are out of the will of God. In fact, quite the opposite. God's will often involves very uncomfortable circumstances. Because of all that has happened with John and his family, my three children have learned that when the unthinkable happens, God is still in control. They saw that as you pray your way through a tragedy step-by-step, God brings good out of the situation. They know that when you walk closely with God and live in obedience to His ways, you can trust that you are in the center of His will, no matter what the circumstances are around you.

This experience and others have made me realize that the center of God's will is not a destination; it's the process itself. God's will is a place we choose to live every day as we seek intimate relationship with the Lord, lay a solid foundation in Him, and learn to walk in His way.

PRAYER

Lord, help me always live in Your way so that I may continually find comfort in the center of Your will.

TOOLS OF TRUTH

The world is passing away, and the lust of it; but he who does the will of God abides forever.

1 JOHN 2:17

Blessed be the God and Father of our Lord Jesus Christ, the Father of mercies and God of all comfort, who comforts us in all our tribulation, that we may be able to comfort those who are in any trouble, with the comfort with which we ourselves are comforted by God.

2 CORINTHIANS 1:3–4

Sing, O heavens!
Be joyful, O earth!
And break out in singing, O mountains!
For the LORD has comforted His people,
And will have mercy on His afflicted.

ISAIAH 49:13

For this reason we also, since the day we heard it, do not cease to pray for you, and to ask that you may be filled with the knowledge of His will in all wisdom and spiritual understanding; that you may have a walk worthy of the Lord, fully pleasing Him, being fruitful in every good work and increasing in the knowledge of God.

COLOSSIANS 1:9–10

NOTES

CHAPTER 2

   1. Joanne Marxhausen, *Three in One* (St. Louis, MO: Concordia, 1973), p. 67.

CHAPTER 14

   1. Oswald Chambers, *My Utmost for His Highest* (Westwood, N.J.: Barbour & Co., 1984), 151.

CHAPTER 21

   1. Chambers, *My Utmost for His Highest*, 177.

NOTES

ABOUT THE AUTHOR

Stormie Omartian is a popular writer, accomplished lyricist, and speaker. She is the best-selling author of ten books, including *Praying God's Will for Your Life Workbook and Journal, The Power of a Praying Wife, The Power of a Praying Parent, Lord, I Want to Be Whole,* and *Stormie,* the story of her journey from the brokenness of being an abused child to becoming a whole person.

A popular media guest, Stormie has appeared on numerous radio and television programs, including *The 700 Club, Parent Talk, Homelife, Crosstalk,* and *Today's Issues.* Stormie speaks all over the United States in churches, women's retreats, and conferences. For twenty years Stormie has been encouraging women to pray for their families. She desires to help others become all that God created them to be, to establish strong family bonds and marriages, and to be instruments of God's love.

Stormie has been married to Grammy-winning record producer Michael Omartian for nearly thirty years. They have three grown children, Christopher, Amanda, and John David.

You can contact Stormie through her Web site:

www.stormieomartian.com

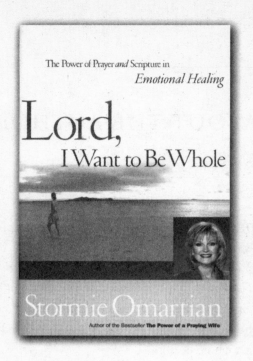

The Power of Prayer *and* Scripture in *Emotional Healing*

Lord,
I Want to Be Whole

Stormie Omartian
Author of the Bestseller **The Power of a Praying Wife**

"Lord, I want to be whole."

These words are the heart-cry of many Christians who, in spite of their relationship with the Lord, find themselves dealing with overwhelming anger, guilt, depression—or perhaps the nagging feeling that something inside them just is not right.

In *Lord, I Want to Be Whole*, Stormie Omartian shares the principles she learned during her struggle for real and lasting peace. What Stormie offers is not a formula for a quick fix but a positive approach that is both spiritual and practical. Her advice and encouragement will help you find—and keep— wholeness in all areas of your life.

978-0-7852-6703-4 • Trade Paper • 256 pages • $14.99